insight text guide

Anica Boulanger-Mashberg

The 7 Stages of Grieving

Wesley Enoch & Deborah Mailman

First published in 2022.

Insight Publications Pty Ltd
3/350 Charman Road
Cheltenham VIC 3192
Australia
Tel: +61 3 8571 4950
Fax: +61 3 8571 0257
Email: books@insightpublications.com.au

www.insightpublications.com.au

A catalogue record for this book is available from the National Library of Australia

Wesley Enoch & Deborah Mailman's The 7 Stages of Grieving / Anica Boulanger-Mashberg

Anica Boulanger-Mashberg asserts the moral right to be identified as the author of this work.

ISBNs:
9781922525260 (print)
9781922525291 (digital)
9781922525307 (bundle: print + digital)

Cover design by Melisa Paredes

Printed in Australia by Ligare Book Printers

contents

CHARACTER MAP

Note that this play revolves around its sole performer's interpretation of the central figure. All the other characters are peripheral, and present only in the Woman's stories. While they are important in her life, we know very little about them and never see them except through her perspective.

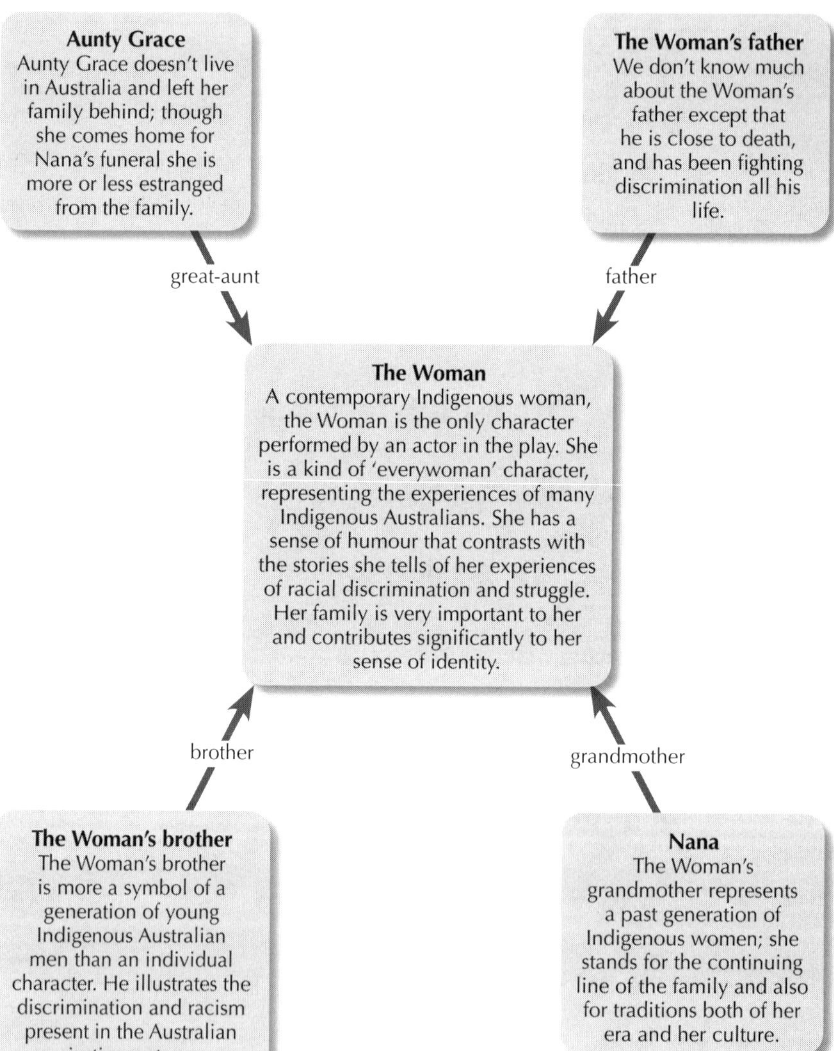

OVERVIEW

Note: In this guide we have chosen to use the term 'Indigenous Australian(s)'. We recognise that there are many differing preferences, and that no single choice satisfies all situations or individuals. Although 'Aboriginal woman' is used in this play, it was last revised (third edition) in 2002 and this usage is no longer preferred. We also recognise that broad terms are not ideal; however, in this play the Woman describes herself only as a 'Murri', a term that may not encompass the wider Indigenous community for whom her story is relevant. While a broader term might be in keeping with the play's narrative, in which the Woman is a kind of 'everywoman' representative of her community, it would also disregard the specificity of her own personal story. In the absence of more specific nationality or language group names, we have instead aimed for consistency in this text guide's discussions. (For more on appropriate language, see 'Vocabulary for writing on *The 7 Stages of Grieving*', pp.66–7.)

About the authors

Wesley Enoch (b.1969) and Deborah Mailman (b.1972) met at the Queensland University of Technology (QUT) when Mailman was studying drama and performing arts, and subsequently the pair worked together to write *The 7 Stages of Grieving* (published 1996); for its first production, in 1995, Enoch was the director and Mailman the performer.

Wesley Enoch has had an extensive career over several decades in the Australian theatre and entertainment industry, working in various capacities, and has written and directed works for many major Australian theatre companies. He has written and/or directed more than thirty works, including productions that have toured nationally and internationally, such as *The Sapphires* by Tony Briggs (dir. 2004). Enoch has won significant awards for playwriting and directing, including the 2000 Matilda Award and the 2001 Deadly Award (celebrating Australian Aboriginal and Torres Strait Islander achievement in music, sport, arts and community) for *The Sunshine Club* and the 2005 Patrick White Playwrights Award for *The Story of the Miracles at Cookie's Table*.

Along with a group of other Indigenous performers and artists, in 1993 he formed the not-for-profit theatrical company Kooemba Jdarra Indigenous Performing Arts in order to tell Indigenous Australian stories, both traditional and contemporary, throughout Australia and overseas. *The 7 Stages of Grieving*, which was first produced by Kooemba Jdarra (1995), was one of his first plays. A Nunukul and Ngugi man (who also has Irish, Danish and Filipino heritage), Enoch continues to produce work that predominantly tells Indigenous Australian stories. He has written and produced adaptations of several canonical European plays, such as *Black Medea* (2000), a version of the ancient Greek tragedy *Medea* (by Euripides) adapted specifically to an Indigenous Australian context.

Although he is best known as a writer/director, he has made notable contributions to Australian theatre and culture in many other roles; for example, he directed the Indigenous section of the 2006 Commonwealth Games Opening Ceremony, and was the director of the Sydney Festival between 2015 and 2021. In 2021, Enoch became the first Indigenous Chair in the Creative Industries at QUT.

In an interview with Ellen Fanning for ABC's One Plus One, Enoch explained that he conceives the role of the artist as being to 'make political change' and to 'create a vocabulary for what the future might be'. He also feels that 'questioning the status quo' is an important duty and that artists can construct a space for voices and stories to be heard; 'by telling stories … also listening to stories, you actually provide a … place that people can grow, can heal, and can make a very *positive* contribution to the world' (Fanning 2019). He considers the roles of artists and storytellers to be significant and important to society, not just entertainment.

Deborah Mailman, a Bidjara woman (who also recognises her Māori heritage), is best known as an actor. She has won industry awards for her stage and screen performances, including Female Actor of the Year at the 2013 Deadly Awards and a 2016 TV Week Logie Award for Most Outstanding Actress for her role in *Redfern Now: Promise Me*. She was also the first Indigenous actress to win the Australian Film Institute Award for Best Performance by an Actress in a Leading Role (for *Radiance* in 1998). She also won the AACTA award for Best Lead Actress in a Television Drama in 2019, for her role in the ABC series *Total Control*.

In 2019 Mailman was appointed to the Screen Australia Board – a recognition of the importance of her voice within the industry and the national narrative. This significant voice can be heard through the words she contributed and performed in *The 7 Stages of Grieving,* offering a contemporary Indigenous female perspective on Australian life. Mailman was also a presenter for several years on ABC television's *Play School,* which, despite being a lighthearted children's show, allowed her to provide an important voice for a new generation of Australians.

The significant cultural and creative contributions of both these artists to their industries has been formally recognised at a high level. Both were made Members of the Order of Australia (AM): Mailman in 2017 for significant service to the performing arts as an actor, and as a role model for Indigenous performers and the community; and Enoch in 2020 for significant service to the performing arts as an Indigenous director and playwright.

Synopsis

The narrative of *The 7 Stages of Grieving* is neither straightforward nor linear. Its short scenes jump through time and space to construct a chronicle of the shared grief of Indigenous Australians. The play is performed by a single actor who tells many stories to weave together a broad perspective of Indigenous Australian history since European settlement that is fraught with loss and destruction. The play shows that contemporary life for Indigenous Australians is not free from this pain, but rather is shaped and informed by it.

In the short scenes the performer (the Woman) tells of family relationships, deaths and funerals, and personal experiences of racial prejudice, interspersed with reactions to the arrival of the First Fleet, Indigenous people's experience of colonialism and Australian society's attempted moves towards reconciliation.

The broad story the play communicates is one of historical loss and dispossession that forms a backdrop for contemporary suffering, damage to identity and vast grief. Although the end of the play suggests that there is hope for the future of Australia in the form of reconciliation, this cautious hope is juxtaposed against the many scenes of loss, pain and distress.

Character summaries

The Woman

The Woman (who is unnamed) is the protagonist. She is an Indigenous Australian woman who has close relationships with members of her family and her extended community.

The Woman's father

The Woman expects her ailing father to die soon, at the age of forty-eight, and she is trying to reconcile herself to his loss in advance.

Nana (the Woman's grandmother)

The Woman's grandmother, Nana, died before the beginning of the play, aged sixty-two, and represents the loss of family and cultural lineage for the Woman.

The Woman's brother

The Woman's brother's experience provides an insight into how easily young men (particularly Indigenous men) can fall into a cycle of crime and conviction, which usually has negative outcomes.

Aunty Grace

After living in London for nearly fifty years, Aunty Grace returns to Australia to attend Nana's funeral. She is almost estranged (though she still remembers some family members' names), and stays in a hotel rather than with family.

BACKGROUND & CONTEXT

Around the time the play was written, in 1995, the Aboriginal and Torres Strait Islander Commission (ATSIC) issued a report stating that recognition of Indigenous Australians in the constitution was a priority. This strengthened the push for constitutional reform. In 1998 a convention to debate the possibility of Australia becoming a republic supported the recognition of Indigenous Australians in a new preamble to the constitution but disagreement about the wording along with the issue of becoming a republic overshadowed the proposal and a subsequent referendum was unsuccessful. The fight for Indigenous recognition in the constitution continued and in May 2000 more than 250 000 people walked across the Sydney Harbour Bridge in support of reconciliation, leading to national demonstrations of support; the addition of Scene 24 to the play was a response to this event.

Two models

The play takes inspiration from two models. The first is Elisabeth Kübler-Ross' 'Five Stages of Grief' model, related both to the experiences of those coming to terms with their own impending death and the experiences of those who become bereaved (Kübler-Ross 1969). The second is a concept of Indigenous Australian history as comprising seven distinct stages, known as 'the seven phases of Aboriginal history'. However, the influence of these neatly staged models does not correspond to a straightforward structure for the play. While, at first glance, the scenes seem clearly delineated and ordered, *The 7 Stages of Grieving* mirrors the stages in Kübler-Ross' original model, which were not designed to be always discrete and sequential, but can be revisited in any order (nor are they all experienced by every person). Similarly, history is never perfectly structured, with every point impacting on the future and reflecting on the past. *The 7 Stages of Grieving* reflects this, in that it is not always clear which stage (of either the five or the seven) is being portrayed in a scene, but all the stages together express the grief the play addresses.

Although it is not vital to have an intricate knowledge of these two models (described in further detail below) in order to understand the play, it is relevant to examine them. These stages of dying and of history link closely with the content of various scenes, as well as hinting at the themes Enoch and Mailman are exploring.

The stages of dying

Elisabeth Kübler-Ross, a Swiss-American psychiatrist, proposed a model of grief whereby the approach to death is described in five separate stages: denial, anger, bargaining, depression and acceptance. In her book *On Death and Dying* (1969), she proposed – based on her work with terminally ill patients – that people experience these five emotional stages as they approach death. Later, with David Kessler, Kübler-Ross adapted the stages of dying to apply to grief. The authors were always very clear that this was a useful model to understand and help manage the experience of loss, rather than a definitive description of what everyone goes through. Indeed, the staged model was not even supposed to describe a particular chronological progression, as many people do not experience every stage, and others will go back and forth between stages at various times.

In terms of the play, the various stages are linked with the themes and issues. For example:

- anger – there is much anger over the past, as seen in Scene 15, when a peaceful march leads to the realisation that Indigenous Australians are having to 'fight most of [their] lives' (p.59)
- bargaining – in the only scene with a title taken directly from the 'Five Stages of Grief' model, the Woman challenges the audience to consider what the land is 'worth' (p.60)

→

- depression – the Woman experiences much depression in the play, from her feelings about her father's impending death to her sorrow over the Stolen Generation's loss of identity and connection to family.

The phases of history

The 'seven phases of Aboriginal history' is a model conceived by Michael Williams (University of Queensland) and has been adopted in this play, but others have similarly proposed various stages in Indigenous history. For example, Ann Curthoys, John Docker and Australian historian Lorenzo Veracini (in the *Australian Humanities Review*) discussed four phases in the philosophical development of Indigenous Australian historiography, with the fourth phase – like Enoch and Mailman's interpretation of the seventh phase – 'still unfinished'. This unfinished stage accommodates the ongoing struggle of drawing together a violent past with the idea of a better future.

The names of the seven phases (Dreaming, Invasion, Genocide, Protection, Assimilation, Self Determination and Reconciliation, as listed on the back cover of the text) each carry many connotations and complex definitions in relation to this play. You will find many of these ideas useful as you analyse the text. As you are reading the play, consider how one or more of these phases illuminates or complicates the scene you are reading. Brainstorm any words, phrases and associations you can think of that relate to each of the named phases – this will be useful as you begin examining themes and ideas and as you write about the text.

Prefatory material

The text includes numerous essays relating to the play. Some of the content may not be relevant to your studies, but you might want to make note of any information in the essays that will help you to form your own interpretations of and contentions regarding *The 7 Stages of Grieving*.

The play is not a long text, containing only short scenes and few characters, but its examination of the experiences of a people and a nation carries many layers of emotion and meaning. By engaging with the prefatory material, you will begin to find ways to understand the many parts of the play that are not necessarily explicitly stated or explored on the page. This is a reminder that no text stands alone but must be read and analysed within a particular context, whether it be the context in which the play was written or that from which you are examining it (and sometimes both). A text like this one, particularly, is rich with cultural and historical assumption that you will need to have some understanding of if you are to analyse the themes and ideas it puts forward.

Below are some examples of ideas that can be drawn from these essays.

'Jagera Land' by Neville Bonner

Ideas include:

- the longevity of Indigenous Australian culture and history
- the importance of narrative and storytelling (p.9).

'Why Do We Applaud' by Wesley Enoch

Ideas include:

- 'faction' (a meeting of fact and fiction) as a genre
- the importance of stories and storytelling: 'When the world was created everything had a story …' (p.13)
- the role of story in traditional Murri culture: 'the story has many ways of being told' (p.14); comment about varied artforms and multiplicity of voice, and discussion of the melding of modes (projection, song, dance etc.) in the play as a 'cultural hybridity' (p.15)

→

- the play as 'a universal theme told through the personal experiences of one character' (p.16) – there is also a kind of link to this in the James Hillman epigraph to the Beaton essay (see below): there is 'no part of my personal record that is not at the same time the record of a community, a society, a nation, an age' (p.17).

'A Story of One's Own' by Hilary Beaton

Kooemba Jdarra produces work by Indigenous creators 'for an Indigenous audience' (p.18) – how does this play sit in that context, and how might audiences connect and respond, especially those who are not Indigenous?

'A Cultural History of Australia'

- Think about the particular dates and details chosen for inclusion in this section – how do they shape your understanding of the text itself? How might other choices have changed your understanding?
- The BP ('before the present') measure is used for time. (Note that once the timeline reaches European contact, the more common dating system of AD is also provided.) How does this shape your perspective, and what do you think is the impact of including AD? Do you think this was a positive/beneficial decision? Why or why not?
- Key terms are introduced here, e.g. Aboriginal Protectorate: a government office, the role ostensibly being to care for Australia's Indigenous peoples.

As an exercise, choose one of the events listed (pp.22–5) and research it. Write a half-page summary of the event and its relevance to this play.

Evolution of the script

Theatre companies across Australia have continued to stage this play over the years – sometimes more than once. The Sydney Theatre Company, for example, staged its fourth production of the play in 2021.

The play was devised as a collaborative work between Enoch as director and Mailman as performer. In numerous interviews and articles since, they have expressed that they always intended the play to shift and adapt to the changing social context in Australia – presumably with some optimism that there would be more positive race relations to reflect in the script as time went on. This adaptation has occurred with the addition of the final scene in this edition, 'Walking Across Bridges', and the later expansion in 2021 to add another scene that solicits tangible activism from its audiences. This shows that a play can be, in some senses, a more mutable text than other forms (such as novels), since each creative team will bring different elements (sometimes even whole new scenes) to their productions of the same script.

GENRE, STRUCTURE & LANGUAGE

Genre

The 7 Stages of Grieving is a **dramatic monologue**: a script written to be performed in a theatre by a single actor. It uses the normal features of theatrical language, such as:

- stage directions (these are particularly important in this play during the scenes that do not contain dialogue)
- sound effects
- props
- sets and set dressing.

The play also uses a multimedia element: the projection of images and words. When you are analysing the play, remember that all of these elements are as important in conveying plot and themes as the words spoken by the actor. Your discussion of themes will be enriched by including analysis of theatrical as well as spoken language.

Although the play is certainly not a comedy, it does incorporate elements of **gallows humour** or **black comedy** (in this instance the word 'black' refers to the dark nature of the humour – do not confuse it with a reference to race). One explicit example is in Scene 12, when the actor is instructed to perform the scene '*in the style of stand up comedy*' (p.52). Other instances of dark humour include the play on words in the scenes 'Wreck / con / silly / nation Poem' and 'Everything Has Its Time', and the use of a humorous tone to refer to a serious event (the arrival of the First Fleet in Australia) in Scene 11, '1788'. Another example is the Woman's observation that death will inevitably come to everyone – notably to those who have been associated with racism (p.46) – a thought that she finds comforting.

These moments of humour work in contrast with the bleak and sorrowful tones in the rest of the play, giving audiences moments of relief, while at the same time emphasising the themes of grief and loss by forcing members of the audience to stop and consider why they are laughing and at what.

Structure

The structure of *The 7 Stages of Grieving* is nonlinear in the sense that the central character does not make a clear chronological progression; instead, the play jumps backward and forward in time. For example, one scene portrays events in 1788 while another recollects the Walk for Reconciliation over the Sydney Harbour Bridge in 2000. Most scenes, however, do not have an explicit temporal setting, offering snapshot-like glimpses of the Woman's life and others' experiences (such as in 'Mugshot').

The play is also written to be performed as one act, which contributes to the intensity of many of its themes: as the Woman's experience of grief and discrimination is relentless, so, too, the emotion of the play is inescapable for its audiences, without the lighthearted relief of an interval.

The scenes are generally short (no more than two pages) while some are very short (just a few sentences). In most cases there is no direct link between the content of one scene and the next, although they are linked more broadly by their exploration of grief, Indigenous history (as well as the contemporary experience) and the interactions between Indigenous and non-Indigenous Australia. As Maryrose Casey and Cathy Craigie have asserted in *A Brief History of Indigenous Australian Contemporary Theatre* (2011), 'traditional Indigenous performance works alternate rhythmically between speech and silence, between the past and the present and between performance and story'. This is a good description of the structure and style of *The 7 Stages of Grieving*.

Each scene has a title in the script, providing a signpost for what the scene conveys – and, in some cases, providing vital context for the scene, such as in '1788'. However, apart from this example, the script does not provide instruction on whether or how the titles should be communicated to an audience during a performance. It is possible that they could be projected onto a screen onstage, as are other images and text in the play, or announced by the actor or a recorded voice. Note that the scene titles at times use poetic and heightened language, such as 'Gallery of Sorrow', forming part of the tone and language of the text as a whole. These are a reminder of the extent to which you need to consider the performance context of the play as you study the text. Elements such as scene titles, stage directions and even the prefatory material create a particular version of the text.

Language

The language choices in *The 7 Stages of Grieving* create a voice that is both naturalistic – relying on colloquialisms of spoken English, informal rhythms and sentence fragments – and literary, using techniques such as repetition, structured rhythm (especially in the poems) and figurative language. As a result, the Woman's vocabulary ranges from informal words and phrasing such as 'Oi. Hey, you! ... Yeh, you ... You're taking up the whole bloody harbour!' (p.50), to the rich emotive language in 'Plea'. Similarly, while their main purpose is to provide practical information to the director and performers (as well as other theatre personnel such as set, costume and lighting designers), the stage directions can also contribute to the text's literary impact by providing supplementary information to readers. The wording of the directions is at times poetic and even figurative in its phrasing and language choices, such as '*her voice assails the audience with a sense of all-encompassing sorrow*' (p.67).

The use of English

Most of the play is written in English, but a number of words throughout come from the Kamilaroi language. These words are integrated into the English lines in a natural way, and context can often give the audience a clear idea of what the word means. Readers of the text also have access to the Glossary (p.75) in order to find a definition. As with the scene titles, in a production this information could be provided for an audience in various ways, such as with a glossary printed in the program.

The two songs in the play are not in English but are 'based on the Kamilaroi language' as researched by Enoch and Mailman (p.74). Translations are not printed in the scenes where they appear, so readers need to seek out the Glossary at the end of the book to find the English meaning of the words.

The two scenes featuring Kamilaroi language occur in the first half of the play, which may suggest that this language and its corresponding culture form the Woman's heritage, both building and underlying her other experiences as an Australian woman. On the other hand, the structural location of the scenes within the play might imply that, as time progresses, these languages are becoming less and less active, just as English becomes the primary mode of communication for the Woman in the latter part of the play. Either reading offers an explanation for the interspersed languages throughout: the Kamilaroi language and the culture it represents are a significant part of the Woman's identity.

Q Why do you think the playwrights decided to present the translations of the lyrics at the end of the text instead of in the scenes in which the songs appear?

Q If you were directing a production of this play, how would you choose to translate (or not to translate) the song lyrics for the audience? Why? What impact would your decision have on the audience's understanding of the play?

SCENE-BY-SCENE ANALYSIS

1 Prologue (p.37)

Summary: *General welcome, with warnings about content that might distress members of the audience.*

This opening scene of the play gives audiences their first glimpse of the physical setting, and the dialogue provides the first hints about the emotional and cultural setting, as well as themes such as death and grief. The set itself is richly symbolic. For example, both 'black' powder and 'white' are described in the set dressing; the choice of these two colours and the relationship between them gives the audience a clear indication of the play's concerns and focus.

By giving this introduction a title – albeit a literal, functional descriptor – and a number, Enoch and Mailman dictate that this short scene is to be considered a part of the play, not simply a pragmatic announcement to facilitate the audience's understanding and enjoyment of the performance.

Q What else do you learn about the play and its single performer/ character from this very short speech?

2 Sobbing (p.39)

Summary: *The sound of a woman crying; words are projected onto one of the screens in the space.*

The character 'Aboriginal Woman' (subsequently called 'the Woman') is named for the first time in the stage directions, some of which (as in the previous scene) are poetic and descriptive; for example, 'alone with her grief' (p.39) is not purely functional and concrete.

The language choices in the stage directions anticipate the style of language in the projected words that follow. There are synonyms (such as 'Pain' and 'Distress' or 'Passion' and 'Love', p.39), there are multiple forms of words (such as the abstract noun 'Grief' and the present tense verb form, 'Grieving', p.39) and there is repetition ('Nothing / Nothing / I feel ... Nothing', p.39). The words are also presented – with the exception of the final line – without any linguistic scaffolding; rather, each is presented on a line of its own as a complete idea. All these ideas are thematically linked to each other, though there are conflicting words too; for example, the word 'love' offers a powerful contrast with the words that express negative and even distressing ideas. The effect of this contrast is to emphasise the importance of each word, particularly those relating to pain.

With the final line, the notion of feeling nothing comes as a shock, leaving the audience questioning why the speaker of these words feels nothing in the face of such grief, pain and suffering. Is it defensive behaviour? Is it forced by someone or something externally, such as the expectations of a situation? Is it an untruth, revealing in fact that the opposite is true: that there is so much emotion it is almost impossible to address? This is one of many instances in the play when audiences are given only sparse or partial information and asked to decode, interpret and even construct meaning for themselves.

Q What other reasons do you think there could be for the speaker feeling nothing?

Q Why do you think this list is presented to the audience in writing rather than being spoken?

3 Purification (p.40)

Summary: *The Woman purifies the space around her and sings a traditional song.*

This is the first of several scenes containing no spoken English. Instead, the dialogue is spoken and sung in an Indigenous language based on the Kamilaroi language, and no translation is offered in the performance or in this section of the text. It is likely that few in the audience will understand the Kamilaroi language, as it is classified as 'critically endangered' by the Endangered Languages Project, meaning that there are no longer any young people speaking the language and it will die along with its elderly speakers, for whom it may not even be their primary language.

The stage directions provide important context for the words and lyrics that follow, as they explain the Woman's actions. These details, however, are not available to the theatre audience, though fire is often recognised as a symbol of purification and the meaning could easily be inferred.

The words themselves are a mix of negative and positive emotions (one phrase a statement of sadness and the other two phrases more optimistic), echoing the contrast presented in the previous scene ('Sobbing') between words for suffering (sorrow, loss etc.) and positive experiences, such as love.

Q If you were directing this play, would you project a translation of the dialogue and song in this scene? Why or why not?

4 Nana's Story (pp.42–3)

Summary: *The Woman relates the story of her grandmother's life and death, and how the family gathered together to mourn her.*

In this scene we have the first taste of extended narrative, which contrasts with the more abstract, symbolic scenes that came previously. 'Nana's Story' offers a literal and logically constructed story of the Woman's grandmother's life, framed by the story of how the family observes her funeral, and references to rituals that celebrate her life. In addition to describing the kind of person Nana was, this story gives insight into the Woman's background, particularly into the importance of family to her, thus introducing one of the text's central themes. Nana was the holder of stories, the Woman says, 'of … who I am' (p.43). The value of stories is another central theme of the text, as, the Woman says, Nana's stories represent 'her life, our traditions, our heritage' (p.43).

Note the use of several well-known euphemisms for death in this scene: 'was taken from us, moved on … passed away' (p.42). This language is striking in a play so heavily focused on grief and loss; we might expect the Woman to be more direct, given that the mourning is described in great detail and with a focus on sensory imagery. On the other hand, this gentler description of death shows that the topic must sometimes be handled carefully and sensitively because it can be so destructive. This language reminds us that parts of the play are symbolic rather than literal.

Key point

The Woman does use the word 'die', but only in reference to Nana's friends, who are somewhat removed from the Woman.

Key vocabulary

Tithe: money paid as a tax to support a religious institution.

Q What do you think the Woman means by 'everyone had their time' (p.42)? How does this illuminate some of the key ideas in the text? Is the meaning always the same when she uses the phrase elsewhere in the script?

Q There are several references to singing in this scene. What role does song play in this text?

5 Photograph Story (pp.44–5)

Summary: *The Woman describes a collection, in her childhood home, of photographs of deceased family members. Some of these photographs are projected to accompany her dialogue.*

This scene portrays a cultural practice of observing a period of time after a person's death, during which neither their name nor their image may be used. In the Woman's house, this means placing their photographs in a suitcase 'till they can be talked of again' (p.44). This scene follows narratively from the previous one, as they take Nana's photograph from the wall and 'without a sound push her into the shadow' (p.44). The language choice here is deliberately emotive, and even figurative. While the scene portrays the tradition of respecting the dead by hiding their name and image, the practice is also subverted, as the play chooses to project these images during the scene, which brings an undertone of discomfort.

The repeated phrase 'everything has its time' at the conclusion of this scene (p.44) links back to the phrase 'everyone had their time' in 'Nana's Story' (p.42). Although the scenes can often feel as though they are separate sections, connections like this (as well as the overall themes and ideas) help to give the play cohesion and flow.

Key point

In this scene, photographs accompany the text. This is another instance when it is important to remember the format of the text: theatre is a visual medium and, while you are primarily studying the written element of the play, you should remember to identify and discuss other theatrical elements where relevant. These photographs should not be confused with the production shots of Deborah Mailman that appear throughout, which are not a part of the play (although they are a part of your text).

Q The first sentence in this scene is a stage direction describing sound effects. How do these sound effects contribute to the impact of the scene?

6 Story of a Father (p.46)

Summary: *The Woman explicitly discusses her thoughts on death and her attempts to prepare herself for her father's imminent death.*

In this scene we move from the death of Nana and of those whose names and photographs have become taboo, to a death that has not yet happened but which casts a deep shadow on the Woman. Physically sitting *'on the edge of the grave'* (p.46) – a place her father inhabits symbolically – the Woman relates her pain at the thought of losing her father. This extreme pain is described in physical terms; long bouts of lonely crying at last lead her to a numbness that blocks the sorrow she is feeling.

However, she also sees that death is an inevitable part of life, and she takes comfort from the fact that 'everyone's got to do it' (p.46). She goes on to list a number of prominent Australian politicians and personalities who are all associated with (or perceived as holding) racist or anti-Indigenous views, policies, statements or actions. 'Philip Ruddick' [sic], for example, refers to Philip Ruddock, Minister for Reconciliation and Aboriginal and Torres Strait Islander Affairs in John Howard's Liberal Government in 2001, who was criticised by some for his attitudes towards Indigenous Australians. By reassuring herself with the inevitable deaths of these figures, the Woman brings a note of humour to the dark scene.

Q The language in this scene contrasts with that in 'Nana's Story', in that it uses the terms 'death' and 'die' several times. What is the effect of this?

7 Front and Centre (p.47)

Summary: *The Woman goes to a funeral and sees a stranger crying. She follows the stranger home and learns that this woman attends many funerals, mourning strangers and hoping to discover her own family.*

The focus on death and grief continues, this time expanding beyond the perspective of the Woman's immediate family. In this scene, the deceased is an unnamed young man, and the loudest mourner is a woman who 'couldn't have known this fella' (p.47). The Woman follows the unknown woman home, which reveals several aspects of her personality: curiosity and confidence.

Q The title for this scene literally refers to the unknown woman sitting in the front row at the funeral. What might it refer to symbolically?

8 Family Gallery (p.47)

Summary: *Images from the suitcase in 'Photograph Story' are projected.*

This scene has no dialogue and does not even feature the Woman. Images seen in 'Photograph Story' are projected again, this time alluding to the many people the Woman has lost throughout her life – perhaps even suggesting that she feels she has lost her sense of self. The images reiterate what the stranger in the previous scene has been missing all her life: biological family. This scene, like 'Photograph Story', is also confronting in that it shows images of deceased people.

Q Why do you think Enoch and Mailman format this scene to stand alone in the script, rather than including it as part of another scene? What is the impact of this on the audience?

9 Black Skin Girl (p.48)

Summary: *Letters are projected onto the Woman's dress as she dances and sings. In trying to escape the letters, she removes her dress.*

This scene also features projection and uses theatrical rather than spoken language to contribute to the growing narrative of the play. This scene is a useful example to discuss when analysing how the mode of the text contributes to its meaning and ideas.

The Woman's singing and dancing are '*childlike*' (p.48) and evocative of a world in which language is not necessary – perhaps a glimpse of her childhood. The projections of letters onto her dress, however, are symbolic of the act of labelling, similar to the way the words of the song label the child as 'black skin girl'. The labelling is inescapable – even when she takes off her dress, the Woman is branded with a letter directly on her skin. The letters are from the Roman alphabet, alluding to the colonial settlement of Australia and the overwriting of Indigenous peoples' languages, such as the one in which the Woman is singing.

Q What decisions might a director make in this scene to help English-speaking audiences understand the song? Consider theatrical language (such as visual components or pace) in your answer.

Q What are other possible interpretations of the use of this alphabet and the song?

10 Invasion Poem (p.49)

Summary: *The Woman, still undressed from the previous scene, performs a poem describing the arrival of European colonisers in Australia.*

The poem in this scene is an extended metaphor describing the European settlement of Australia as a violent intrusion of strangers into a person's home. The story is told in the first person, making the images especially confronting, as they refer specifically to the character immediately before the audience: the Woman. By extension, the poem breeds empathy for the Indigenous population of Australia who suffered violence and lost their home and land at the hands of the invading settlers.

The language in the poem shifts from friendly ('smiling', 'offering', 'invited', 'listened', 'soft', 'led') to violent ('chained', 'stolen', 'wrenched', 'forced', 'silenced', 'unsympathetic'), contributing to the vivid imagery as the Woman describes the 'invasion' of her house and the destruction of her family. The imagery in the poem is more confronting because the Woman is still naked and vulnerable from the previous scene. This is an example of how the spoken text of a play can be enhanced by visual elements of performance.

Q At the beginning of this scene, very specific sound effects are described in the stage directions. Why do you think Enoch and Mailman have chosen these particular sounds? How do they relate to what is happening in the play at this point? For each sound, provide at least one association or symbolic meaning.

11 1788 (p.50)

Summary: *The Woman tells the invading settlers not to stay.*

This short scene offers another metaphorical description of European settlement, though in a completely different style. There is no explicit indication that this is what the Woman is talking about; however, the scene title, '1788' (projected for the audience's benefit), paired with the mention of the harbour makes it clear that the scene is referencing the arrival of the First Fleet. The quotation marks around the dialogue indicate that the Woman is quoting someone else's words – presumably an imagined Indigenous person witnessing the European invasion, though the language and attitude is contemporary. While the tone of the short speech is comical, the underlying meaning is not. The audience understands that, in the real, historical version of events, the Indigenous residents of the land did not manage to wave off the fleet. The Woman's casual, dismissive and amusing accusation, which treats the invaders like a troublesome neighbour, belies the seriousness of the issue.

12 Murri Gets a Dress (pp.52–3)

Summary: *The Woman buys a new dress and describes her experiences of everyday discrimination.*

This scene marks a significant shift in the tone of the play, using comedy as a counterpoint to the austere scenes of grief and suffering. As happens elsewhere in the play, the previous scene has already introduced the shift in tone, guiding the audience away from the emotional intensity of 'Invasion Poem'. However, the comedy in this scene is masking an equally bleak contemporary story, as the Woman experiences several forms of discrimination in almost every part of her day. The scene is delivered *'in the style of stand up comedy'* (p.52), which invites audiences to laugh by using various techniques, including the following.

- Subversion of expectation: the first speech contains a common comic lead-in inviting the audience to recognise a shared experience, though the irony is that the experience may not be common to all: 'you're black'.
- Repetition: the phrase 'nice hair, beautiful black skin, white shiny teeth' recurs several times, acting as a comic refrain.
- Toilet humour: someone in the elevator farts ('someone boodgi', p.52).

The scene also uses phrasing and terms from Indigenous English (such as 'deadly', meaning excellent) to contribute to the construction of the Woman's character and the sense that she is creating humour at her own expense.

13 Aunty Grace (pp.54–5)

Summary: *The Woman's Aunty Grace returns home from London for Nana's funeral.*

The Woman does not remember meeting her Aunty Grace, and is intrigued when she arrives for Nana's funeral. Aunty Grace is described as being almost completely alienated from the family, although when she arrives she impresses the Woman by 'remembering names … and guessing ages' (p.54). Although she has been distanced from the family for almost five decades, she still resembles them: 'she fit in to the look of us all' (p.54), an indication that biological family will always be connected, no matter what.

Key point

Aunty Grace represents two ways of defining family. One is by inescapable physiological, biological similarity (she looks like others in the family), and the other is social choice (she has moved overseas and been isolated from the family). The tension between these two aspects is notable at various points in the play.

Aunty Grace doesn't cry over Nana's death until the end of the scene. Her way of grieving is different from the rest of the family's and she is judged accordingly, demonstrating further that she does not share emotional links with the family. However, when she does grieve, the stagecraft is used to visually link her emotion to other instances of grief: her crying is connected viscerally to the suitcase and the sand, both central symbolic elements of the Woman's journey throughout.

14 Mugshot (pp.56–7)

Summary: *The Woman describes an incident in which a group of youths in Brisbane provokes the attention of police, who chase and arrest them, ultimately leading to the death of one of the young people.*

The Woman reports this dramatic incident in a formal way, '*with no hint of emotion*' (p.56) – a significant contrast with the tone in many other scenes. This creates tension between the emotional content and the emotionless delivery. For the majority of the scene, the Woman is reading the report from a piece of paper, indicating that the information has come from elsewhere. Language choices, especially for the description of the more violent moments in the anecdote, are clinical, abrupt, concise and concrete. For example, Daniel Vocke ('known as Boonie', p.57) is 'intercepted' before his arrest; he 'went to the ground' (p.56) in a scuffle during the arrest, and is later described as 'remaining on the ground for some time' (p.57).

There are also significant moments when the Woman breaks from the tone and the 'script' of the report, reminding us of her emotional connection to the scene and the reality of its content.

Note that at no point does the description include the youths' race; their Indigenous identity is implied by the context. This illustrates the importance of considering sections of the text as part of a larger whole, rather than as separate incidents or moments in characters' lives.

Q Although the Woman relates this story with no emotion, it is clear what she feels about the events and where her sympathies lie. How does the play convey this? (Consider language choices as well as theatrical elements such as stage directions, facial expressions and timing of delivery.)

Q Why do you think the stage directions instruct the performer to *'[break] away'* from the written page and *'improvise the text in her own words'* (p.57)?

15 March (pp.58–9)

Summary: *In response to the death of Daniel Vocke, 6000 Indigenous Australians participate in a peaceful march in Brisbane city.*

The opening of this scene, *'The Woman stands strong'* (p.58), offers an immediate contrast with the sorrowful ending to the previous one. The scene does not describe the exact reason for the march, but due to its location in the play and the meeting place of 'Musgrave Park', where the youths met in the previous scene, it can be read as a protest against deaths of Indigenous Australians in custody, particularly the death of Boonie. However, the scene could also be read as an assertion of defiance against systemic prejudice and disadvantage. Although the Woman initially reiterates that it is a 'peaceful march' and 'we're not fighting, we're grieving' (p.58), by the end of the march she cries, 'Don't tell me we're not fighting! Don't tell me we don't fight most of our lives' (p.59). This is a reminder of the play's themes of racism and discrimination, which are constants for Indigenous Australians.

In contrast to the previous scene, here emotional, descriptive language and imagery convey the feelings the Woman is experiencing. Sentence fragments and juxtaposed short and long sentences convey the sense of being overwhelmed. The language also draws on imagery relating to the senses, giving the audience a visceral connection to the scene. For example, the Woman describes the silence, broken only by 'the shuffle of shoes' (p.58), and then the vivid 'clapsticks, the singing, the clapping, the pounding of our feet and the piercing ring of whistles' (p.59). Repetition also contributes to the increasing intensity of the march, such as when she builds on the phrase, 'I'm in a crowd', adding a new phrase with each repetition (p.58). This also imitates the rhythm of marching.

16 Bargaining (p.60)

Summary: *The Woman plants a 'for sale' sign in the red earth on the stage.*

In this short scene (contrasted against the longer scenes before and after), the Woman acknowledges bitterly that her traditional land and history are being taken away from her. Her rhetorical question invites us to consider whether it is possible to put a financial value on history and culture, and forces the audience to confront the fact that non-Indigenous Australia has treated Indigenous Australia like an anonymous property that is on the market. Note that the sign implies a purchase – some form of exchange in which the Woman would receive payment when her land and history are 'sold'. However, in this play we see that it is a theft and not a sale that dispossesses the Indigenous community.

Q This is the only scene with a title taken from one of the 'Stages of Grief' or 'phases of Aboriginal history'. Why do you think this is the case?

17 Home Story (pp.61–3)

Summary: *The Woman uses some of the earth on the stage to tell a story about family relations and rules regarding marriage.*

The earth in this scene takes on a new symbolism; it represents family as well as how family relates to 'the land, the source, the spirit, the core of everything' and to 'culture … song, tradition, dance' (p.61). This scene brings a little humour back to the narrative with the repetition and confusion of which 'mob' is which, and the complex relationships between who is part of one's family and who one is allowed to marry according to traditional 'skin' laws. Family here includes cousins and grandparents as well as immediate family. In this conception of family, 'every one has their place' (p.61) and it is vital to understand family relations in order to navigate your own identity.

In stark contrast to the lighthearted lesson in family law, the final lines and gesture cut through the tone of the scene; the Woman says, 'Now imagine when the children are taken away from this', and physically destroys the family diagram in the earth (p.63). Having demonstrated the complexity and importance of knowing your own family, the Woman now confronts audiences with the reality of the Stolen Generation; we are forced to imagine the extent of the damage done by removing children from their intricate web of family connection and identity.

In this scene, the Woman addresses the audience, using the second-person pronoun 'you', regularly asking, 'Are you with me?' Although the whole play is based on the Woman telling her story, this is one of the few scenes in which she addresses the audience directly. (Note that in '1788', although she uses 'you', this does not refer to the audience but to the imagined invaders in the scene.) This has the effect of increasing the connection between the Woman and the audience as she breaks the traditional 'fourth wall' of theatre (the separation and lack of interaction between actors and audience), while also forcing audience members to feel complicit as they assess their own role in the Australian cultural landscape. The final repetition of 'Are you with me?' asks audiences not only whether they have followed the logic of her complicated story of skin relations, but also whether they are her allies or not.

18 Story of a Brother (pp.64–5)

Summary: *The Woman tells the story of her brother's criminal history, when he fell into a cycle of conviction and shame.*

The Woman's story of her brother is more detailed than the story of her father in Scene 6, but both are equally bleak. In this story, she shows how a series of small incidents quickly escalates into serious criminal convictions. She also describes how easily the shame of conviction can spiral into a cycle of poverty and increase the possibility of being repeatedly convicted, painting a picture of hopelessness. As the scene ends, the family is still in suspense, anticipating the next step in this depressing cycle. Nothing in the monologue gives the audience any reason to believe that anything positive will happen.

Key point

The narrative in this scene recalls the story in 'Mugshot' and reminds us that interactions between Indigenous peoples and the upholders of non-Indigenous law can be devastating: 'to be shamed out like that eats your spirit, your life' (p.65). By juxtaposing the processes of non-Indigenous law with those of Indigenous cultural law (in the previous scene), the play hints that the two are incompatible.

Q Why do you think this scene begins with '*the sound of laughter*'?

19 Gallery of Sorrow (p.66)

Summary: *The 'phases of Aboriginal History' are presented; there is no dialogue.*

Another wordless scene (similar to 'Family Gallery') provides the audience with time to digest the meaning of the previous scene. However, the absence of dialogue does not mean the scene is a passive one. This is one of few scenes that directly refers to the 'phases of Aboriginal History' (p.66). The stage directions list the seven phases and specify that they are to be represented through images, but as they are explicitly named, a director might also choose to present the titles of each verbally, such as by projecting them on the stage.

Q The later 'phases of Aboriginal History' could be seen as positive developments ('*Self-determination*' and '*Reconciliation*'). Why do you think the scene is titled 'Gallery of Sorrow'?

Q If you were directing this play, what would you ask the actor to do during this scene, and why?

20 Suitcase Opening (p.67)

Summary: *The Woman paints herself and then opens the suitcase.*

This scene is also wordless, except when the Woman's voice '*assails the audience*' (p.67), conveying deep sorrow in the tone of the previous scene. As in other scenes without dialogue, it is important to pay attention to the physical objects and images, as they carry symbolism that can help you in your understanding of the play as a whole. In this scene, the significant symbols are land, people and family, emphasised in three different ways: they are mentioned in the stage directions, conveyed in the earth and photographs and shown in the projected images.

Q Curiously, there are no lines of dialogue to explain how the Woman's voice might be 'assailing'. What do you think might allow her to use her voice?

Q Why do you think the Woman paints herself '*as if preparing for war*' in this scene, before she grieves?

Q As a director, how would you convey the '*catharsis and release*' at the end of the scene?

21 Wreck / con / silly / nation Poem (p.69)

Summary: *A poem plays on the word 'reconciliation'.*

In this scene the contrast between the childlike wordplay (emphasised by the words projected in a *'childlike script'*) and the deep sorrow underlying the poem creates a tension that again reminds the audience that grieving is one of the central experiences for the Woman and for many of her fellow Indigenous Australians. This grief comes not just from the pain caused by those in her immediate family (her worry for both her father and brother and her sense of loss over Nana and other family members), but also from the history of what has been committed against her people. In this scene, the word 'reconciliation' – which has positive connotations of compassion, resolution and healing – is twisted to become a group of words with negative meanings. These words are communicated in a poem that reflects the cruelty and devastation of colonisation, and the ongoing 'mess' of contemporary Indigenous/non-Indigenous relations.

Q How is the poem in this scene similar to the poem in Scene 10? How do they differ? What does this tell you about the journey the Woman takes throughout the play?

Q The scene is about grief and loss. Why do you think the Woman begins the scene *'cleansed, fresh'*?

22 Everything Has Its Time (p.70)

Summary: *The Woman continues to play with the word 'reconciliation'.*

Carrying on from the previous scene, the Woman repeats the negative words created out of the syllables for 'reconciliation'. This shows how the seemingly simple idea of Indigenous and non-Indigenous Australians reconciling with each other is not simple at all, but carries complex connotations, challenges and problems. The Woman implores us to 'think and talk about' the word. This scene reminds us of the difference between word and action; though *'the space is full of words'* (p.70), only action – not just talking – will change lives.

This scene could be interpreted as carrying more hope than many other scenes in the play, with the repeated line that also forms the title: 'Everything has its time' (p.70). This suggests that while there is much grief and suffering still to be navigated, a positive, reconciled future is a possibility.

Key point

Note that, in the Glossary for this text, the word 'reconciliation' has been included, but the definition offered is, 'what does it really mean?' (p.75). The play insistently asks us to consider what the concept of reconciliation means and how it can be enacted.

The title of this scene first appears as the closing words of 'Photograph Story', the fifth scene, in which the Woman talks about the suitcase that contains photographs and memories of departed family members. Here, the suitcase makes a reappearance: *'the word RECONCILIATION is packed into it'* (p.70). The title also recalls a line in 'Nana's Story' describing how the family mourns for Nana – 'everyone had their time' (p.42). These echoes of mourning and a funeral help reiterate that the scene is also about loss and grieving.

23 Plea (p.71)

Summary: *The Woman describes the depth of her grief and offers her people's stories to the audience.*

As the play concludes, the Woman links her own grief with that of her people, and she offers the suitcase and all it contains – land, stories, people, family, sorrow – to her audience. She describes how her people's grief has been muted and hidden, which has contributed to the need to tell the stories of Indigenous history and of the contemporary experience.

In speaking directly to the audience, the Woman ensures that the intensity of her feelings is communicated forcefully; the audience cannot look away or ignore her stories and the stories of her people. As with 'Home Story', she implicates the audience in the narrative journey of the play. In placing the suitcase before the audience, she hands over responsibility for carrying and understanding these stories.

24 Walking Across Bridges (pp.72–3)

Summary: *The Woman describes the Walks for Reconciliation across Australian bridges.*

The title in this scene has several meanings.

- Literally, it describes the walk across the Sydney Harbour Bridge (and, later, across other bridges in Australia) in the name of reconciliation.
- Metaphorically, it recalls the idiom, 'we'll cross that bridge when we come to it', alluding to the appropriate time to deal with a problem.
- Symbolically, it refers to 'bridges' (links) that are beginning to be constructed and traversed between Indigenous and non-Indigenous Australians as part of the process of reconciliation.
- Also symbolically, bridges represent the transition from past to future as Australians actively begin to acknowledge wrongs of the past and attempt to move on to a better future.

The descriptions of the bridge walk recall the march in Scene 15. As the Woman describes the mass of people and the 'tingle' she experienced both at the time and in the recollection, she also draws a symbolic reference to Indigenous culture with the description of the crowd as being 'like a rainbow serpent' – a deity referenced in many Indigenous stories and often alluded to colloquially as representing Indigenous culture and story. This helps bring the play to a close with a note of optimism for the future.

Q Do you think the hopefulness in this scene seems realistic given the heavy emphasis on grief throughout the rest of the play? Why or why not?

Q The play was first produced in 1995 and this scene was added in the 2002 edition of the script. If you had to write a new scene today, what would you add to represent any changes in culture since 2002?

CHARACTERS & RELATIONSHIPS

The 7 Stages of Grieving is an unusual text because it has very few characters and, apart from the Woman, those it does contain are present only in descriptions (and occasionally images) mediated through the Woman's perspective. In this way, the narrative voice of the text resembles that of a first-person or a third-person-limited point of view in a novel or short story.

Although the play is a **monologue**, meaning only one actor speaks throughout, the Woman does talk about other characters. These are discussed briefly below, though they are more important for how they relate to the themes of the play than how they are developed as characters. With the exception of Nana and brief mentions of other family members, these characters only appear in single scenes.

The play could be read, at times, as a single actor playing various roles; for example, the stand-up comedy scene (Scene 12) could be delivered by the performer playing a different character, as the stage directions do not specify that it is the Woman delivering the lines. However, this guide takes a reading that one character, the Woman, tells many stories – some directly hers (such as 'Photograph Story' or 'Aunty Grace') and others from a broader or different perspective, or even in a different mode ('Invasion Poem', 'Murri Gets a Dress', 'Mugshot'). This makes her a character who represents the lives and journeys of many people who share characteristics with her. This also reflects the play's construction: although it contains elements of both Deborah Mailman's and Wesley Enoch's experience, it is not an autobiography.

Characterisation

In most texts, characters are carefully developed as unique individuals with particular stories to tell and journeys to follow. Authors use techniques such as vocabulary choice, style and tone to differentiate between characters. In *The 7 Stages of Grieving,* however, one single character tells all of the stories that make up the text, and language is used more to convey tone and mood than to construct character. The Woman is characterised more by her feelings and her desires than by words or actions, and in many ways we do not come to know her well by the end of the play.

Often the characters the Woman describes are not differentiated as individuals either. When she talks about her grandmother's funeral, for example, she speaks of traditional customs, such as the instruction not to wear black at a funeral or the moment when 'the boys painted up and danced' (p.43), rather than identifying the attendees. She describes the many family members present at the funeral as a generic group rather than as individuals: 'someone would start singing along' (p.42); 'the gathering, the old aunties, the uncles' (p.43); 'black fellas as far as the eye could see' (p.43). So while there are many different characters peopling the play, and some (such as Aunty Grace) are constructed uniquely, there are many more who appear as shadowy figures at the periphery of her story, filling out the scenes but not necessarily shedding any light on the main protagonist.

We know only minimal information about the secondary characters in the play, with little detail about their behaviour, values or decisions. Rather, they tend to stand as representatives of various aspects of the Woman's life: generally community, culture and grief.

The Woman

Key quotes

'I miss my grandmother. She took so many stories with her to the grave.' (p.43)

'Sometimes I find myself crying in the dark alone … I cry and cry until I can't feel anymore.' (p.46)

'I'M … BLACK! AND DEADLY!' (p.53)

'Don't tell me we don't fight most of our lives.' (p.59)

The Woman is a kind of 'everywoman' Indigenous character, representing a life and a set of experiences that belong to many in her community, rather than being distinguished as a unique character. This is apparent from the fact that she has not been given a name – although 'Woman' is capitalised when referring to her, showing that she does have some individual identity and is not an entirely anonymous figure. While her own experience is central to the play, it is not central in the way it would be in a more conventional narrative, where a main protagonist shapes the narrative arc of the text as they grow and change through the events of the plot. The Woman does not take a traditional narrative journey with clear crisis points or significant changes and development. Rather, she is a voice for a bigger story, and her purpose is to paint for the audience a portrait of where contemporary Australians stand in relation to Indigenous history.

Key point

Unlike most protagonists in traditional texts, the Woman has not changed significantly by the end of the text. Each scene shows a moment in her reality, but as a whole the play presents a series of snapshots rather than a narrative arc.

Despite the fact that the Woman is in some ways merely a representative of a group, she still has distinct features and qualities. For example, she has a sense of humour that emerges at several key moments of the play, such as during the representation of the 1788 arrival of the First Fleet and the 'Murri Gets a Dress' stand-up comedy scene. She uses humour to convey her reality – in 'Murri Gets a Dress', for example, she demonstrates the daily struggles and discrimination a contemporary Indigenous woman faces.

We also know she takes an active and interested role in the world around her. This is demonstrated by moments such as that in 'Front and Centre', when she follows the 'old Aunty' (p.47) home from the funeral to find out more about her, as well as the way she speaks of others, such as the depth of detail she uses to describe her Aunty Grace.

Although the Woman struggles with racial discrimination and finding her identity in contemporary Australia, she also has confidence and resilience, as is displayed in 'Murri Gets a Dress'. She is pleased with how she looks in her new dress ('looking pretty deadly', p.52) and is not concerned when she locks her keys in the car, but instead demonstrates her resourcefulness ('this Murri too good', p.52). Even after the series of frustrating events in her day, and after being called 'fat' by an aunty, the next day she still sees herself as beautiful and 'DEADLY!' (p.53).

The Woman also cares deeply about her family – one of the play's central themes – and the role family plays in her own identity. When the Woman's grandmother dies, Nana takes with her not just 'many stories' but a sense of the Woman's heritage and who she is (p.43). Specific scenes are dedicated to her father, brother, Nana and aunt, as well as to her extended family in 'Photograph Story' and the wordless 'Family Gallery'.

The Woman's father

Key quote

'… he hasn't stopped fighting since 1967.' (p.46)

As well as representing immediate family, the Woman's father represents an immediate past that she is grateful she will 'never have to live through' (p.46). Only forty-eight years old, he is 'in and out of hospital' and the Woman knows he does not have very much time left to live (p.46). He cannot rest – even though he knows he should – because he 'hasn't stopped fighting' (p.46), presumably, for Indigenous recognition and rights. The Woman identifies the beginning of his fight as 1967, in which year a constitutional referendum was held to officially recognise Aboriginal and Torres Strait Islander people as part of the Australian population. Her father represents the ongoing fight against society's racism.

Although she does not detail her father's health conditions or disclose why he is dying, the fact that he is already nearing the end of his life at the age of forty-eight alludes to the reality that life expectancy for Indigenous Australians is significantly lower than that for non-Indigenous Australians – yet another form of inequality between the two groups. As in a number of other instances, these details are not given explicitly to the audience; the play relies on some contextual knowledge of setting and content.

Nana

Key quotes

'My grandmother was a strong god-fearing woman who, at the age of 62, was taken from us, moved on … passed away.' (p.42)

'She was a woman who couldn't trust doctors, a woman who couldn't speak to teachers or police, wouldn't answer the telephone, gave her tithe to the church and got nervous at the mention of the "gubberment".' (p.42)

The Woman's grandmother, who died at the age of sixty-two, represents the generation before the Woman's father; her role in the text is even more directly related to grief and mourning, since her introduction early in the play is through her own funeral. 'Nana's Story' (Scene 4) gives explicit descriptions of the kind of woman Nana was, as well as providing the Woman's subjective view of what Nana meant to her.

In the second key quote above, we learn a great deal about the kind of woman Nana was, yet many of these characteristics and qualities could be common to a whole generation of Indigenous Australians. Her similarity to others is suggested by the fact that all the old aunties and uncles sing together after the service, a song unfamiliar to the younger generations. This is a symbol of the common culture and experiences Nana shared with her contemporaries.

The Woman's brother

Key quote

'Now this fella, my brother, he's not the smartest of men and when he's on the charge … he can be a little clumsy … So with his sense of justice and him sticking up for his Bungies, he pushed the police officer …' (p.64)

Similar to Nana, the Woman's brother represents a common experience for his demographic (young Indigenous men). The Woman describes how little it took for her brother to become trapped in the vicious circle of the criminal justice system after he tries to stand up for a friend. The Woman describes her brother's deep shame at being arrested, which in turn brings shame on the family. She reminds us that these experiences are common: 'it can happen to anyone' and 'we've seen it too many times, cousins going in and then you get that call' (p.65). Though there is ambiguity in this last sentence, it is possible the Woman is alluding to cases of death in custody – a major concern for her brother and his family if he goes to jail. A Royal Commission into Aboriginal Deaths in Custody was conducted at the end of the 1980s, so the issue was particularly relevant not long before this play was first performed.

Her brother is the only sibling who is allocated some space in the Woman's story. We know the Woman has a sister, for example (p.43, p.58), but there are only brief mentions of her. In 'Nana's Story', her sister is mentioned as someone who was very close to their Nana and who saw Nana's death coming (signifying the strength of family bonds, and also the permeating experience of grief throughout the play), but we do not encounter her again, suggesting that the Woman's relationship with her sister is not as significant for her as other relationships.

Aunty Grace

Key quotes

'... though she looked like no one in particular from the family, she fit in to the look of us all.' (p.54)

'Now I'm a Christian woman and I forgive her but ... No more. No more talking of her.' (Nana, p.54)

Aunty Grace represents a group of Indigenous peoples that we do not encounter in the rest of the play: those who have left Australia (and thus their families, community and culture) by choice. Though she returns for Nana's funeral, her immediate family has always considered her a deserter and they don't exhibit any affection for her. However, Aunty Grace seems to have kept up with the family from afar, 'remembering names ... and guessing ages' (p.54). She is isolated from her family to the extent that photographs of her are 'only brought out on request' (p.54), just as photographs of the deceased are hidden; Nana forbids talking about her again, as it is forbidden to speak of the dead.

Aunty Grace does not show her grief in the same way as the rest of the family, reminding us that there are many ways to grieve. When she finally does break down and cry at Nana's grave, the Woman describes this moment with accompanying physical action that connects with symbolism elsewhere in the play: both the suitcase and the red earth are used as props connecting Aunty Grace back to her family and culture.

THEMES, IDEAS & VALUES

Community

Key quotes

'The whole family came together for meals.' (p.42)

'I never knew my family – maybe I could meet my real family …' (p.47)

The Woman in *The 7 Stages of Grieving* is part of several specific communities; one defined by her genetic identity and another largely defined by her Indigenous identity.

Family

Family forms an intimate level of community defined by blood relations. The Woman's close immediate family includes her brother, father and grandmother; her mother is barely mentioned, so may not be a key figure in her life. There is a second circle of family that includes her Aunty Grace. Finally, she has a wide extended family who are unnamed – her sisters, 'young cousins' (p.42), 'old aunties, the uncles' (p.43) and the circle of community beyond this, whether or not they are related biologically: 'black fellas as far as the eye could see' (p.43). For the Woman, family helps shape her identity. Nana and her stories define her ('who I am'), and after Nana's death she feels as though this identity is 'gone' (p.43).

The frequent use of photographs in the play also emphasises the importance of family. The suitcase of photographs is featured in a number of scenes, including 'Photograph Story' and 'Family Gallery', both of which include projections of the images. This nonverbal textual element is a way of underscoring the theme that is explored elsewhere in dialogue. For example, the scene 'Family Gallery' contains no dialogue at all, but still powerfully conveys the notion that family is a significant influence on individuals' lives and identities. Similarly, in 'Suitcase

Opening', any dialogue is replaced by the photographs, symbolising not just family but the connection of family to the broader world: *'images of landscape interweave with family portraits creating a tapestry of Land and People'* (p.67).

In 'Front and Centre' (Scene 7), the Woman repeatedly mentions that the young man who died 'had no family to speak of' (p.47), yet the Woman has attended his funeral, as has the stranger, the 'old Aunty' who the Woman later follows home. This suggests that, in the absence of direct family, there are other ways communities draw together. This scene, however, also reiterates the importance of family, as the old Aunty goes to funeral after funeral hoping to meet her 'real family', whom she never knew. To be without family is, for her, a source of grief. Thus, the text values family as a protective and supportive force in individuals' lives.

The play also shows that, along with positive contributions to individuals' lives, familial relationships can also lead to grief (a central idea in the text). For example, in 'Story of a Brother' (Scene 18) we see how the arrest of the Woman's brother sends waves of distress through not only him but the whole family. They experience shame at his treatment, and, the Woman says, 'in our family to be shamed out like that eats your spirit, your life' (p.65). Closeness can breed pain, and the actions of one family member can damage the lives of others.

There is one character in the play who represents the idea that biological connection cannot always hold people together. Aunty Grace has separated herself from her family – 'upped and left us' (p.54) – and they turn away from her in response: 'Dad said she was stuck up and wasn't really family' (p.54). Her decisions and actions have alienated her from the strong family connections positively illustrated elsewhere in the play. This shows that, while one's family relationships are intense and important, they are not immune to dissolution.

Non-biological connections

Blood relations are not the only communities represented in the play, as the Woman perceives herself to be part of a community larger than her own family. The play is primarily about her existence as an Indigenous Australian, and her 'everywoman' role shows that her experiences are shared by many others. One of the ways in which she indicates that she is part of this sector of society is her frequent use of the inclusive pronouns 'we' and 'us', and corresponding language such as 'our'. For example:

- Nana is 'taken from us' (p.42)
- at Nana's funeral, the songs of the hundreds of attendees 'soared above us' (p.43)
- during 'March', the thousands of peaceful protesters/mourners unite as a crowd – 'we come from a long tradition of storytelling', 'we rise' and 'we're not yelling, we're not fighting. We're grieving' (p.59)
- her sarcastic remark, 'you know how we all look alike' (p.64)
- 'we have been taught to cry quietly … only our eyes betray us' (p.71).

In addition to the language choices, the settings of various scenes paint strong portraits of the power of community. In several scenes, for example, the Woman describes herself as part of a group – she joins the mourners in 'Nana's Story' ('Black fellas as far as the eye could see', p.43) and also in 'March' ('I'm in a crowd … everyone just walks together', p.58) – while, in the final scene, the community has widened to encompass non-Indigenous Australians also. As the conclusion of the play, this scene offers an arresting image of the possibility of a future where equality unites community. The woman gets a 'tingle' remembering the 'over 1/4 of a million people … walking across bridges' in a symbolic march of hope – hope born of a sense of togetherness (pp.72–3).

Structured community

One scene in particular shows the ways in which community roles, relationships and rules can be regulated, and how they can determine an individual's rights and restrictions. 'Home Story' (Scene 17) is an explicit explanation of the way that conventions and laws define the options within the Indigenous community. The Woman's tongue-in-cheek narration in this scene illustrates the complexities of community structures and relationships, poking fun at the rules that govern who she can and cannot marry. The prop (the soil) allows her to visually demonstrate what she is explaining, and to show the fragility of family and community boundaries. Although it is meant to be a funny scene, it ends with a fierce physical illustration of the devastation caused when community is destroyed – in this case, she is alluding to the Stolen Generation.

Key point

Note the contrast in this scene between the seriousness of the content and the humorous tone of the speech. This is similar to the juxtapositions in '1788' and 'Murri Gets a Dress', during which humour draws the audience in while also highlighting the seriousness of the material.

Race relations in Australia

Key quotes

'My children, stolen away …
The protests of my mother's mother cut short …
Told not to do what we have always done.' (p.49)

'They've written sorry … (Pause) … they've written sorry across the sky.' (p.72)

The 7 Stages of Grieving relentlessly shows its audience the devastating impact of both historical and contemporary dispossession, damage and prejudice against Indigenous Australians perpetuated by non-Indigenous Australians, whether colonial settler-invaders or contemporary citizens.

There are few representations of positive interactions and dynamics between races – the interactions are absent (such as in 'Photograph Story'), powerfully negative (such as in 'Invasion Poem' and 'Murri Gets a Dress'), implied (such as in '1788', which is a direct metaphor; or 'Front and Centre', in which the stranger's disconnection from her family might suggest she has been part of the Stolen Generation), or they simply provide a background for the rest of the Woman's story (such as in 'Story of a Father'). Race relations intimately underlie the entire play – whether explicit or not – since the theme of Indigenous dispossession and discrimination is the backbone of the text.

The one positive representation of Australian race relations is the short scene concluding the play, which is one of cautious optimism and hope. It is given narrative weight due to its structural positioning, as it is the final impression left with the audience. Similarly, as the sole scene showing hope for a unified future Australia, it is impactful because it stands out from the rest of the play. However, the fact that it is the only hopeful scene means that its impact is also undermined: while there may be hope, it is barely accessible beneath the relentless grief portrayed.

Key point

This scene was added in an updated edition of the play, written much later than the original text, in order to acknowledge some progress towards reconciliation.

History

The play presents, in several scenes, interpretations of the history of non-Indigenous arrival, settlement and colonisation of the land that is now Australia. Primarily, these scenes are:

- Invasion Poem (Scene 10)
- 1788 (Scene 11)
- Bargaining (Scene 16)
- Gallery of Sorrow (Scene 19)
- Wreck / con / silly / nation Poem (Scene 21).

In each of these scenes, the Woman conveys opinions and feelings intended to be generalised to a wide range of people from the many Indigenous nations that were colonised by Europeans. These are some of the scenes in which she is most like an 'everywoman' character, telling a story that she is part of but that is not distinguished by her own unique experience. In these scenes, with the exception of 'Invasion Poem', she does not use the first-person pronoun as she does elsewhere in the play (e.g. when she tells the story of Nana's funeral). This reminds us that she is not describing isolated events but rather a national history and narrative that has repercussions for all Australians. In 'Invasion Poem', although using the first-person 'I', she is not really referring to herself but rather using herself as a metaphor for all Indigenous Australians, just as 'the front door' does not refer to a literal house but to the country itself (p.49).

Even when she does tell her own personal stories – such as in 'Murri Gets a Dress' or 'Story of a Brother' – using first-person pronouns and events and settings specific to her own life, audiences are expected to extrapolate from these scenes an understanding of the experiences of an entire community and not just one woman. For example, in 'Murri Gets a Dress', the Woman describes herself as 'black', and her sardonic line, 'You get a lot of attention, special treatment when you're black' (p.52), is not intended to describe just the shopping excursion that is the focus of the scene; it describes a broader experience of discrimination. Similarly, at the end of this scene, when she goes to bed hoping that 'tomorrow will be a better day' (p.53), the audience understands that this also represents a (perhaps unwarranted, given the preceding events) persistent optimism about the future of Indigenous Australia. Equally, the fact that she wakes up 'STILL BLACK' (p.53) suggests that the battle against discrimination is a constant one. Interestingly, though, the character at this moment is not downtrodden by the endless struggle, as she is in other scenes, but rather celebrates her identity: 'I'M STILL BLACK! AND DEADLY!' (p.53). This complicates the notion that Indigenous Australians are merely defending themselves against omnipresent discrimination, showing that there is still pride as well as grief stemming from Indigenous identity.

Discrimination

The play offers a number of very specific illustrations of the discrimination faced by the Woman (and by extension many, if not all, Indigenous Australians) on a daily basis. When Nana dies, the Woman tells us that she was 'a woman who couldn't trust doctors, a woman who couldn't speak to teachers or police ... and got nervous at the mention of the "gubberment"' (p.42). While the Woman does not say that the reasons for these characteristics were Nana's Indigenous identity, it is indicated by the use of the word 'couldn't' rather than 'wouldn't' – Nana was not just stubborn but had *reason* not to interact with the authorities and institutional figureheads. Her culture has been forcibly assimilated into non-Indigenous Australian systemic values and structures, and she has likely faced discrimination as a part of this.

'Murri Gets a Dress' is one of the most explicit depictions of everyday racism and discrimination in the play. The Woman's story in this scene illustrates how her every action is judged, how her very appearance prompts bias and generalised assumptions, and the extent to which she is shown disrespect for no reason. At the shop it is implied that she will steal or cause damage. When she locks herself out of her car, it is assumed that she is breaking into someone else's. When her car breaks down, no one stops to help her, almost certainly because she is 'black'. Note that the text does not need to say why the cars drive past her; the context tells us that this is yet another incident in the relentless catalogue of discrimination. Even when someone farts in the lift, the Woman is blamed, showing that discrimination is the norm not only in significant situations but even in trivial events.

This default prejudice is echoed in 'Story of a Brother', where the Woman's brother becomes incidentally caught up in a criminal arrest, prompted by the fact that the police have mixed up one 'black kid' with another (p.64). The brother is volatile and reactive, fulfilling police expectations (based on the colour of his skin) of his behaviour, and he immediately falls into a cycle of delinquency and reoffending that will continue to shape not just his own life but also that of his family.

Disempowerment

Along with discrimination can come a loss of agency – or, equally damagingly, a perception of such disempowerment.

In *The 7 Stages of Grieving*, the Woman struggles to find a place in a world that does not recognise her identity and her connection to country. As a result, she fluctuates between a sense of strength and place within her community – such as with her pride in 'Murri Gets a Dress' – and an inability to maintain her inner strength in the face of insistent attacks on her value and identity.

Identity

Key quotes

'Have you ever been black?' (p.52)

'My **Nation** knows my identity …' (p.69)

Much of the Woman's sense of self is intertwined with her Indigenous identity and her place in a cultural community and, in turn, that community's place within broader society. This idea is introduced early in the play, when the Woman mourns her Nana's death, grieving not just for the loss of a loved one, but also for the loss of a central pillar in the Woman's sense of who she is and where she fits into the world. Nana and her songs and stories represent not just 'traditions' and 'heritage', but actually, the Woman says, 'who I am' (p.43) – this part of her is so closely tied to her Nana that, at her death, the Woman's identity is 'gone'. This is echoed in the 'Nothing / Nothing … Nothing' that the Woman feels as a culmination of her suffering (p.39) – her emotional toil is so relentless that she sometimes feels totally stripped of her sense of identity.

The Woman, in her narrative role as a symbol of the Indigenous peoples of Australia, is frequently forced to integrate into the non-Indigenous society around her, meaning that her deeply held commitment to her Indigenous heritage is constantly challenged and undermined. For example, as 'Invasion Poem' symbolically describes, the Woman and her community have been forced to 'feed upon another tongue', as they are stripped of their language (p.49). Their voices are 'silenced' as they are 'told not to speak, not to dance. / Told not to do what we have always done' (p.49). It is unimaginable that one's identity could stand up to such a systematic crushing; the best a person could possibly hope for would be to incorporate a dominating identity into an existing and historical identity. The Woman, to an extent, is able to do this – we see her holding onto her birth identity in the two scenes comprising entirely Kamilaroi language ('Purification' and 'Black Skin Girl'). These scenes are not directly translated for audiences of the play, suggesting that there are ways in which the Woman is able to maintain the side of herself that she connects with her family and her heritage.

As well as the Woman's positive connection with her family (as in 'Nana's Story'), there are negative experiences that shape the family and the way it sees itself, such as the brother's situation, which affects the Woman's perception of herself in particular: in her family, shame 'eats your spirit, your life', leaving a void of some kind in her beliefs about herself (p.65). Similarly, the colour of her skin is something that visibly defines her, and she seems to have an ambivalent relationship with it. While she is proud of this identity, which she calls 'DEADLY' (p.53), she also suffers under the weight of a society that constantly judges her for it, and so it is also a symbol of her fears that her 'heart is hardening' (p.71).

The line 'have you ever been black?' (p.52) has complex layers of meaning in terms of identity. In the context of the scene, which is '*delivered in the style of stand up comedy*' (p.52), a line like this is intended to draw in audiences and invite them to share the experience of the comedian, thus heightening the comedic impact of the observation about to be revealed. Yet this play does not assume an exclusively Indigenous audience, so the question can also be viewed as being provocative – the implied answer, for many audience members, is 'no'. Thus the scene is her way of conveying to us what it is like to be her: what her identity feels like from her own perspective, not just from the perspective of those who judge her from the outside.

Hopelessness

Key quotes

'I feel ... Nothing.' (p.39)

'It's inevitable, death.' (p.46)

'I go to bed thinking "Tomorrow will be a better day"…' (p.53)

'What a mess.' (p.69)

The play portrays a woman and a people who have been insistently and violently oppressed, dismissed, judged, demonised and taken advantage of. A consequence of this is to explore to what extent hope can be found in such situations. Overwhelmingly, the play shows that there is more hopelessness, but that there are small ways of resisting and of finding hope. Still, the notion of a kind of reconciled freedom is rarely presented as being possible, let alone likely. Instead, principally, we are shown over and over that people cannot escape such treatment.

Struggle and repression

Many scenes show the extent to which the Woman and those around her struggle to stay afloat under such difficult circumstances. The scene 'Sobbing' hints that, even before the play has properly begun, the Woman has, to an extent, given up in response to the long list of emotional challenges catalogued in the scene. Worn down by the constant struggle to survive these challenges, through distress and pain she has begun to feel numb, to feel 'nothing' (p.39). This early introduction to her suffering shows us just how overpowering the daily pressures of life can be. Structurally positioned early in the play, the scene also introduces themes, concerns and emotional tones to be addressed in the text.

The Woman has also seen her family, before her, endure such struggles, which must make it even more difficult to maintain any hope of a better future. Nana was afraid of going to hospital, didn't trust the medical, justice or education systems to have her best interests at heart, and was frightened by what the 'gubberment' might do next to control her life (p.42). The Woman's father, equally, has been 'fighting since 1967' – the year when a constitutional referendum resulted in changes to the laws governing the rights of Aboriginal and Torres Strait Islander peoples (p.46). This shows that he has had to persistently stand up for his rights, but the scene ('Story of a Father') suggests that he has also been fighting battles at a personal level for many years, dealing with an unnamed health condition from which his daughter expects he will soon die. Although she tries to reassure herself that she might not have to fight some of those same battles – 'I'll never have to live through what my Dad lived through' (p.46) – there is an overarching sense of hopelessness in this scene, characterised by the tone of grief and the focus on mortality.

Another way in which the play demonstrates the entrenched sense of hopelessness in Australia's unequal society is in the later scenes about reconciliation (or 'wreck / con / silly / nation'). The Woman shows little optimism that any social change is possible, or even that there might be any form of recognition of what she and her people have been through. She wonders, 'What's the use in having a word if we don't think and talk about it' (p.70). This suggests a despondency about the potential for reconciliation, despite the fact that the scene is called 'Everything Has Its Time', suggesting that reconciliation will have its time, too.

Resilience and resistance

Despite what may seem to be the insurmountable challenges of fighting against a society intent on supressing, devaluing and destroying her culture, the Woman finds moments of optimism in the narrative, and the play communicates this to us in several ways. One of these is through humour, with which the Woman shows us that she is able to retain a core of strength despite the discrimination and cruelty the world throws at her. The most obvious example of this is in 'Murri Gets a Dress', when she delivers her story '*in the style of stand up comedy*' (p.52), self-consciously harnessing humour to underscore the intensity of the discrimination towards Indigenous peoples. Through the humour we see that, even faced with other people's negative assumptions about her, she is proud of who she is and feels good about her resilience in a hostile world. Another example is the wry humour of '1788', in which the comedic impact of the scene is to remind us of the injustice of the colonial invasion. In this case the humour does not so much serve to illustrate resilience but to show that, despite the challenges, people are sometimes still able to make jokes, even at their own expense, and use this not just as a coping mechanism but a way to draw others to them.

The play also shows that strength can be found in numbers. For example, the peaceful protest in 'March' offers a portrait of some degree of power under difficult circumstances; it shows a situation in which the community is able to gather together to '*defiantly*' tell its story (p.59). This scene also acknowledges a strength that can come from having to 'fight most of our lives' (p.59). And while the second scene ('Sobbing') describes '*an Aboriginal Woman alone with her grief*' (p.39), the play increasingly shows the shared grief of a whole culture, and thus reminds us that glimmers of hope may also come from being surrounded by a strong community.

The 2002 insertion of the final scene, 'Walking Across Bridges', cuts across some of the despair explored elsewhere in the play. The scene, one of hope, can be read as a kind of reply to Scene 22, 'Everything Has Its Time', in which the word 'RECONCILIATION' is '*packed into*' a suitcase as though for a day in the distant future when it might become usable (p.70). The action in 'Walking Across Bridges' responds to the act of packing images of the deceased into the suitcase much earlier in the text, as with Nana in 'Photograph Story'. There is a complex symbolism at play here. While the act of putting an image or an idea into a suitcase represents acknowledgement that it has passed away and is no longer accessible to the living, we also know that this is a temporary rather than permanent banishment: there will come a time in the future when this stage of grieving has ended, when 'they can be talked of again' (p.44). Just as this is true of relatives who have died, 'Walking Across Bridges' shows us that this is true of the notion of reconciliation. The idea was once packed into a suitcase but now is being brought out into the open. While the play does not have a conventional happy ending, it concludes by showing us a glimpse of a future where some of the suffering of the past may be taken from the darkness of its suitcase, to be addressed (possibly even redressed) in the lives of the living.

DIFFERENT INTERPRETATIONS

Different interpretations arise from different responses to a text. Over time, a text will evoke a wide range of responses from its readers, who may come from various social or cultural groups and live in very different places and historical periods. Responses by critics and reviewers can be published in newspapers, journals and books, both online and in print. They can also be expressed in discussions among readers in the media, classrooms, book groups and so on.

While there is no single correct reading or interpretation of a text, it is important to understand that an interpretation is more than a personal opinion – it is the justification of a point of view on the text. To present an interpretation of a text based on your point of view, you must use a logical argument and support it with relevant evidence from the text.

A play is open to the shifting influence of interpretation in a more penetrable way than a printed text such as a novel or collection of poetry, or even other forms such as film. This is because each individual production of a play may incorporate many elements that are not explicitly visible in the script. This will present a production company's interpretation (by emphasising certain elements or connections between elements), which in turn will influence the audience's and critics' interpretations. Examples include features of the genre such as set, props, lighting, staging (or 'blocking', which is the direction and choreography of the actors' movements on stage), costumes and, especially, direction and performance – the way the actors deliver lines. An actor's delivery includes pitch, pace, rhythm, emphasis and vocal tone. While many of these features may be suggested in stage directions in the script, stage directions are not always intended to be strictly adhered to and individual productions may vary.

Another way in which a play is open to new interpretation is with script revisions or the inclusion of new material. This happened in the 2002 production of *The 7 Stages of Grieving*, with the addition of

'Walking Across Bridges'. This new scene shows how context can change the interpretation of a text: the writers wanted to incorporate new events that had occurred since the first performance and publication of the script. This additional material sheds new light on some of the themes and ideas in the play and allows us to interpret different meaning from the text.

In the 2021 Sydney Theatre Company (STC) production of the play, director Shari Sebbens (along with actor Elaine Crombie and Assistant Director Ian Michael, and with the approval of Enoch and Mailman) added an 'epilogue' scene, acknowledging significant social change in the decades since the bridge walks for reconciliation. The epilogue engages the audience more assertively and tangibly in the play, integrating a call for what Steve Dow in *The Guardian* has labelled 'activism' (Dow 2021). This interpretation concentrates on the need for motivated action in order to convert the gradual progressive move towards social change into much more decisive shifts in attitudes to race in Australia.

It is also possible to demonstrate subjective interpretations in more subtle ways, such as with the inclusion of new material in the form of words not spoken by the actor. For example, in the same STC production, during the scene 'Mugshot', the names and dates of Indigenous deaths in custody since the play's genesis were projected onto the screen behind the actor. This interpretation emphasised the ongoing relevance of the play, showing that, although it is more than twenty-five years old, the content is not historical but contemporary: stories like that of 'Boonie' are still happening. Note that this contemporary material was integrated into the performance in a way that acknowledges and respects central aspects of the original text. This is apparent not just in the content of the new material but also, importantly, in its style and form. The projection of dates and names echoes the original production's projection of images of the many family members who have died (such as in 'Photograph Story' and 'Family Gallery'). This is a reminder that an 'interpretation' must be closely connected to, and supported by, the text itself.

Many older plays are performed using the full original script but this can be a kind of interpretation, too – presenting old ideas in a new context in order to draw audiences' attention to the timelessness of particular issues or, alternatively, the ways that society has changed. Some productions that retain the original script might alter the context radically. (An example is Baz Luhrmann's 1996 film *William Shakespeare's Romeo + Juliet*.) This allows the director to emphasise particular aspects of the play.

It is interesting to note that several productions of *The 7 Stages of Grieving* have elected to add new material rather than simply adapting setting, style or even the medium.

The critics' viewpoints

As Enoch notes in his foreword to the 2002 edition of the play, critical reception of the first production was mixed, with not all audiences or reviewers appreciating it. Over time, this has changed, with positive reviews dominating the responses to various productions in recent years.

But a theatre review is not simply a positive or negative evaluation; rather, it is a discussion of the text and performance from a particular perspective. This may mean that the review concentrates more on the script, or on the production or particular actor's performance, or on one particular aspect of the text. In the case of *The 7 Stages of Grieving*, many theatrical reviews respond particularly to the individual production, and generally focus on the sociopolitical concerns of the play, responding to the issues of Australian race relations that it examines. The issue of Indigenous suffering has remained deeply relevant since the play's first production, but the social context has also changed, as is evidenced by some of the new material added to the script to reflect significant events such as the bridge walks for reconciliation.

However, in her review in the *Canberra Times* of the STC's 2021 production (their fourth production of the play over the years since it first opened), Sally Pryor notes that 'the sad truth is that not a lot has changed in the 26 years' and that its themes are 'still depressingly relevant today' (Pryor 2021); her interpretation of the text is that it tells a story reminding us of the lack of change in ongoing discrimination against the first peoples of Australia. Although she acknowledges the new closing scene, one designed to instil more hope in its audience, she shows no evidence that she has been convinced by this attempt. Steve Dow in *The Guardian* similarly feels that the play is 'deeply and depressingly politically relevant' still (Dow 2021), and stresses that the new epilogue is a vital addition, really hammering home the idea that, rather than seeing positive change over the life of the play, the past twenty-one years have been full of setbacks. On the other hand, in her review of the same production for *Time Out*, Debbie Zhou seems more inspired by the attempts at optimism in the play: the final scene's 'veer to activism burns hopeful' (Zhou 2021).

Melissa Lucashenko's 2015 essay for Copyright Agency's 'Reading Australia' examines the hope in the play, the movement towards a more promising future. She believes that, with their play, Mailman and Enoch were offering the audience a 'way forward' and 'the possibility of reconciliation' (Lucashenko 2015), noting that the play's second season was better received than the first, identifying change in the audience's social context. Although she notes soberly that, in some ways, little has changed for Indigenous Australians, in other ways she thinks there has been significant forward movement, as evidenced by the increased visibility of the issues, such as through Indigenous artists Enoch and Mailman's increased recognition in the Australian entertainment industry.

Although the role of a theatre director is not to critique a play, direction and production form an interpretation of the text just as a critic does. For Shari Sebbens (director of the STC's 2021 production), the idea of moving forward contrasts with the bleak impressions of the critics above; she asks how audiences can consider the 'devastating' material while 'not being appalled and shocked that between each production, in some aspects we've gone backwards'. Rather than a depressing conclusion that nothing has changed since the play's first production, she asks her audience to find hope and to actively commit to a future where 'this play doesn't need to be done in another ten years?' or 'if it is, it's a conscious and deliberate look back at the past — as opposed to a sad indictment of our present' (Bremer 2021).

Two interpretations

Interpretation 1: *The 7 Stages of Grieving* is an embodiment of irreconcilable hopelessness.

The play offers us countless reasons to lose hope in our world and our society. The Woman suffers unyieldingly, whether from the assaults on her culture and community (both historical and contemporary), the incessant discrimination against her and her family, or her own personal griefs – unrelated to race – such as the soul-destroying death of her grandmother (Nana). Even the moments of humour in the play are gallows humour, illustrating hurtful and damaging situations and events. In '1788', she shouts humorously at an imagined vehicle parking where it shouldn't; the scene is clearly a metaphor for the European invasion of the land that would become Australia. In 'Murri Gets a Dress', the actor is instructed to deliver the lines '*in the style of stand up comedy*' (p.52), but even though the Woman shows pride and pleasure in her own black and 'deadly' identity, this comic monologue is contrasted with the daily racism and violence that she is subjected to. This humour uses irony to emphasise the underlying grief, despair and disparity between one race and another.

The 7 Stages of Grieving, based on a psychological model of grief, death and dying, as well as on a theoretical model of the traumatic history of white invasion and black suffering in Australia, insists that we, as a culture, are guilty of not making progress in creating change. Thus those who are discriminated against and devalued have no reason to hope the future might bring such change. The final scene, added to the play years after its initial production, attempts to show some hope for reconciliation in the future, but this is the sole scene, out of twenty-four, offering any positive perspective on Australia's capacity to amend past wrongs and work towards a stronger, unified future.

The sections of the play that explore the Woman's own personal story, too, feel saturated in hopelessness. She grieves her grandmother's death, taking with it as it does not just 'traditions' and 'heritage' but also, she says, 'who I am' (p.43) – the Woman's very identity. Later, she views her father only as someone who has struggled for decades and is now ready to die – an impending event she attempts desperately to cope with. Her Aunty Grace is practically estranged from the family, representing more sorrow and loss. 'Story of a Brother' paints a grim picture of a cycle of violence and conviction, with little sign that there is any way to break that cycle. Again and again, we see the misery in this woman's life, and the lack of optimism about any possible change to her situation.

Interpretation 2: Despite the grief and futility permeating *The 7 Stages of Grieving*, the Woman shows us strength and possibility.

The 7 Stages of Grieving addresses themes and ideas that are bleak and paint a portrait of a racist and ignorant Australia that disrespects and damages its Indigenous peoples. The Woman is a symbol of the damage done historically and of continuing hatred and discrimination. Yet, importantly, what the play shows us is that there is strength in survival and in persistent resistance against a system that aims to repress. The Woman is often resilient in the face of the prejudice she is constantly subjected to. For example, in the scene 'Murri Gets a Dress', she describes several incidents of ignorant and bigoted behaviour directed at her by white characters and authorities. While the scene shows us the grim experiences of a Murri woman in contemporary Australia, it does so with comedy, which is a way to illustrate the power of the Woman: she is able to turn the scene around so that it ridicules those doing the discriminating, and ends with her victorious pride in who she is and how 'deadly' she is. Although the final paragraph contains clear irony – it is not likely for her that 'tomorrow will be a better day' (p.53) – the scene's final words, in all capitals for emphasis, resoundingly celebrate the Woman's strength and ability to survive what is thrown at her.

We also see optimism in the Woman's solidarity with her community. While there is conflict between Indigenous and non-Indigenous Australians, there is rarely any between the members of the Woman's own family and wider community. The peaceful protest in 'March' shows the comfort that can be found among members of a united community, even in the face of terrible grief. The protest becomes a space to demonstrate defiance and a commitment to the fact that they all have to 'fight most of [their] lives' (p.59) – we see that they will not have to fight alone.

Finally, the last scene of the play (added to reflect optimistic change in Australian society) offers encouraging evidence that circumstances are changing and that reconciliation is possible. The Woman describes, with awe, the 2000 bridge marches through which Australians offered apology for past wrongs and committed to building an inclusive and united future. The closing words – 'I guess we can't go back now' (p.73) – convince us that society is moving forward, away from the racial violence and denigration that has dominated non-Indigenous interactions with Indigenous peoples for too long. Ultimately, the play ends on a note of great hope.

QUESTIONS & ANSWERS

This section focuses on your own analytical writing on the text, and gives you strategies for producing high quality responses in your coursework and exam essays.

Essay writing – an overview

An essay on a literary work is a formal and serious piece of writing that presents your point of view on the text, usually in response to a given topic. Your 'point of view' in an essay is your interpretation of the meaning of the text's language, structure, characters, situations and events, supported by detailed analysis of textual evidence.

Analyse – don't summarise

In your essays it is important to avoid simply summarising what happens in a text.

- A **summary** is a description or paraphrase (retelling in different words) of the characters and events. For example: 'Macbeth has a horrifying vision of a dagger dripping with blood before he goes to murder King Duncan.'
- An **analysis** is an explanation of the real meaning or significance that lies 'beneath' the text's words (and images, for a film). For example: 'Macbeth's vision of a bloody dagger shows how deeply uneasy he is about the violent act he is contemplating, and conveys his sense that supernatural forces are impelling him to act.'

A limited amount of summary is sometimes necessary to let your reader know which part of the text you wish to discuss. However, always keep this to a minimum and follow it immediately with your analysis of what this part of the text is really telling us.

Plan your essay

Carefully plan your essay so that you have a clear idea of what you are going to say. The plan ensures that your ideas flow logically, that your argument remains consistent and that you stay on the topic. An essay plan should be a list of **brief dot points** covering no more than half a page.

- Include your central argument or main contention – a concise statement of your overall response to the topic.
- Write three or four dot points for each paragraph, indicating the main idea and evidence/examples from the text. Note that in your essay you will need to *expand* on these points and *analyse* the evidence.

Structure your essay

An essay is a complete, self-contained piece of writing. It has a clear beginning (the introduction), middle (several body paragraphs) and end (the last paragraph or conclusion). It must also have a central argument that runs throughout, linking each paragraph to form a coherent whole. See examples of introductions and conclusions in the 'Analysing a sample topic' and 'Sample answer' sections.

The introduction establishes your overall response to the topic. It includes your main contention and outlines the main evidence you will refer to in the course of the essay. Write your introduction *after* you have done a plan and *before* you write the rest of the essay.

The body paragraphs argue your case – they present evidence from the text and explain how this evidence supports your argument. Each body paragraph needs:

- a strong **topic sentence** (usually the first sentence) that states the main point being made in the paragraph
- **evidence** from the text, including some brief quotations
- **analysis** of the textual evidence, with **explanation** of its significance and how it supports your argument
- **links back to the topic** in one or more statements, usually towards the end of the paragraph.

Connect the body paragraphs so that your discussion flows smoothly. Use some linking words and phrases such as 'similarly' and 'on the other hand', though don't start every paragraph like this. Another strategy is to use a significant word from the last sentence of one paragraph in the first sentence of the next.

Use key terms from the topic – or synonyms for them – throughout, so the relevance of your discussion to the topic is always clear.

The conclusion ties everything together and finishes the essay. It includes strong statements that emphasise your central argument and provide a clear response to the topic.

Avoid simply restating the points made earlier in the essay – this will end on a very flat note and imply that you have run out of ideas and vocabulary. The conclusion should be a logical extension of what you have written, not just a repetition or summary of it. Writing an effective conclusion can be a challenge. Try using these tips:

- Start by linking back to the final sentence of the second-last paragraph – this helps your writing to flow, rather than leaping back to your main contention straight away.
- Use synonyms and expressions with equivalent meanings to vary your vocabulary. This allows you to reinforce your line of argument without being repetitive.
- When planning your essay, think of one or two broad statements or observations about the text's wider meaning. These should be related to the topic and your overall argument. Keep them for the conclusion, since they will give you something 'new' to say but still follow logically from your discussion. The introduction will be focused on the topic, but the conclusion can present a wider view of the text.

Essay topics

1. Discuss the notion of 'silence' in *The 7 Stages of Grieving*.
2. How do Enoch and Mailman use multimodal elements to develop themes in the play?
3. "This fella's done nothing wrong."
   How does *The 7 Stages of Grieving* explore the idea of injustice?
4. 'Despite the fact that the play is a monologue, we learn little about the protagonist's motivations and growth.' Discuss.
5. 'The individual is nothing without family.'
   To what extent do you agree?
6. 'The play begins with a funeral but ends with hope.'
   Discuss the way Enoch and Mailman use structure to convey ideas.
7. 'The Woman's identity is formed through suffering.' Discuss.
8. "I miss my grandmother. She took so many stories with her to the grave."
   What role does story play in the text?
9. 'The play intends to shame non-Indigenous audiences.'
   To what extent do you agree?
10. "We're not fighting, we're grieving."
    Discuss the role of loss in the play.

Vocabulary for writing on *The 7 Stages of Grieving*

Everywoman / everyman character: A character in a text who is designed to reflect the shared experience of humanity or of a particular section of humanity. In *The 7 Stages of Grieving* the Woman (her lack of a unique name gives us the hint that she is an everywoman character) stands in for the experiences of a whole generation of Indigenous Australians.

Indigenous and non-Indigenous: When discussing issues in this text relating to race, it is important to maintain sensitivity regarding terminology. (Also see 'Overview', p.1.) Although Enoch and Mailman, for example, might use 'black' as a non-judgemental term for 'Indigenous' in the play, this is sometimes acceptable for Indigenous speakers in a way that it may not be for outsiders to the culture. In some cases it is only considered acceptable to use this term if you are a member of the community concerned. Also note that the prefaces to the play are dated, using terms such as 'Aborigine', which is no longer an acceptable term. If you want to use particular terms, you may wish to discuss these with your teacher first.

Monologue: Lines in a play delivered by a single actor, alone, either directly or indirectly communicating with the audience.

Murri: A general term to refer to an Indigenous person from particular areas in New South Wales and Queensland.

Nonlinear structure: A complex narrative structure that does not simply progress chronologically from one event to the next.

Reconciliation: In the Australian context, the notion of bringing together Indigenous and non-Indigenous Australia, particularly by recognising past wrongs committed by European settler-invaders. The Woman plays with interpretations and meanings of this word, identifying the negative connotations instead of the positive. (See particularly 'Wreck / con / silly / nation Poem' and 'Everything Has Its Time'.)

Analysing a sample topic

Discuss the notion of 'silence' in *The 7 Stages of Grieving*.

Always be sure that you understand your topic well before you begin to draft your essay. There are many ways to address this topic. One is to begin by defining all the key words – look up dictionary definitions and then translate those into your own words to ensure that you clearly understand their meaning. In this topic, the main key word is 'silence'. 'Discuss', another key word, is an instruction, telling you what form your essay should take – you are not being asked to argue for or against a certain statement. Rather, 'discuss' invites you to consider the topic from many angles, without necessarily taking a position on it. However, you will still need a main contention, as this is what shapes your research and writing, and without one your essay will lack structure and logic.

For this topic, your contention will need to show how you intend to narrow down your ideas on the key concept – silence is a very broad idea and you need to focus specifically on its representation and purpose in this particular text. One way to narrow down ideas is to start by brainstorming as many ideas as you can. Jot down everything you think of when you read the word 'silence': what does it mean to you? (This can include connotations and personal connections, not just the literal dictionary definition.) What are some synonyms? What other notions is it associated with (e.g. calmness, tension, lack of freedom, potential, loneliness, absence)? Under what circumstances might silence be observed or experienced? Can you think of any metaphors involving silence? What are its positive and negative connotations? How might you use the word in an unusual or unexpected way?

Once you have played with all these ideas, you will very quickly be able to eliminate those that are less relevant to this text, leaving you with some to focus on. For example, you might look at three ideas: silence as pervasive; silence as repressive; silence as respectful. These can be turned into your main contention, such as: 'In *The 7 Stages of Grieving*, the idea of silence is everywhere, and it is shown to be both damaging and healing.' Once you have a main contention, it will help you to break your ideas into paragraphs, and to find supporting evidence from the text – remember that, in a multimodal text, evidence is not always in the form of dialogue. It may be provided in stage directions, set descriptions or other non-spoken elements.

Sample introduction

> *The 7 Stages of Grieving* uses the notion of silence to both communicate and illustrate its central narrative, that of the dispossession of a people. Wesley Enoch and Deborah Mailman use literal silence in the play – for instance, in scenes that have no dialogue – as well as figurative silence, principally in the forms of death and loss, to portray the grief alluded to in the play's title. Silence represents the absence of voice and agency; it represents the solitude of grief, but it also sometimes represents power, such as the power to bring people together – beyond language – to begin to heal.

Body paragraph outline

Paragraph 1

The notion of silence is pervasive in the text, being represented in various ways.

- Some scenes are silent (with no dialogue, though sometimes with other sounds or music), such as 'Gallery of Sorrow' or 'Family Gallery'. This forces the audience to viscerally experience the weight of silence.
- Silence is often figurative: at the end of 'Sobbing' (p.39), the Woman says, 'I feel … Nothing', and, later, 'I cry and cry until I can't feel anymore. Numbed. Nothing' (p.46). These words express a kind of emotional silence.
- Silence is also associated with other concepts explored in the play, such as – from the list in 'Sobbing' – loss, death, emptiness, despair, loneliness, absence and desolation.
- At times silence is shown to be protective, and draws people together (as in 'March').

Paragraph 2

Silence is often represented in the text as a form of repression or destruction.

- In this text, the history of the Indigenous peoples of Australia is presented as a history of silence: of an entire culture being silenced – the Woman's (figurative) mother was 'silenced by a single wave of a stick' (p.49).
- The death of the Woman's Nana (the 'silencing' of a life) leaves her with an absence of the stories that make up her heritage and even her identity / sense of self.
- Even in their grief, Indigenous Australian peoples have been 'taught to cry quietly', not to show their real emotions – '*the Woman* places the Suitcase down at the feet of the audience', begging them to undo the silencing of a culture, to give '[her] people's stories' a voice (p.71).

Paragraph 3

Silence is not always a completely negative notion/experience in the play.

- In 'Photograph Story', while the dead are silenced and their family too are silenced because they cannot speak the names of those who have died, the Woman says 'everything has its time'. This silence is a form of respectful grieving, and will not be permanent.
- After the death in 'Mugshot', the community undertakes 'a peaceful march, a silent march'; 'people all walking along in silence ... No one speaks' (p.58). The silent grief is a way of mourning together as a community, and coming together in strength even when they must 'fight most of [their] lives' (p.59); in a way this silence ironically gives people a voice.
- In the final scene (the only scene showing real hope for reconciliation) the Woman is reflecting on the bridge walk, using just one form of sensory imagery – sight – and does not report any dialogue or any sound made by the walkers; although they were

surely not silent, she creates the image of a future opening up and building unity with no need for words.

- In this final scene, there are no stage directions describing any sound effects: instead, there are numerous and frequent pauses between the Woman's lines – uncommon elsewhere in the play – that give us a space, in the silence, to imagine the wondrous sight she is describing.

Sample conclusion

> Silence is a motif that draws the nonlinear play – which is constructed in a series of scenes not always obviously linked to each other – into a coherent whole. It is presented in the form of physical silence in the theatre, as reported silence at events the Woman describes, and as the figurative silence of death and grief. By revisiting this idea in various ways, *The 7 Stages of Grieving* makes a strong and enduring connection between silence and the central theme of the play: grief.

SAMPLE ANSWER

How do Enoch and Mailman use multimodal elements to develop themes in the play?

In the multimodal text *The 7 Stages of Grieving*, Wesley Enoch and Deborah Mailman employ elements such as poetry, song, sound effects, lighting and visual projection to augment the spoken language of the play. They layer these techniques together to enrich the meaning of the script, aiding understanding of ideas, heightening the emotional impact of scenes and deepening the power of the themes they explore, including grief and the absence of reconciliation in Australia. The multimodal elements are sometimes used in concrete ways to underscore the events happening in the spoken content, and at other times they may be more abstract, symbolically reiterating points that are being made in other modes.

From the first scene, Enoch and Mailman harness theatrical elements such as stage design and set dressing. The *'black powder'* of the main performance area is *'framed by a scrape of white'*. The use of the colours black and white is, of course, not coincidental in a play exploring relationships between different races. Furthermore, the main area is black while the white presence is merely a thin 'scrape'. This carries numerous connotations – such as the fact that the Indigenous history of Australia is an extremely long one, while European history in Australia, in comparison, is very brief – and also alerts us to the fact that the story we are about to be told is one mainly of Indigenous Australian experience, and of the way that a white Australian context dictates that experience.

The multimodal elements of this text are often used in very literal ways, to aid our understanding of the script's concerns. For example in the scene 'Home Story', since the story is 'very complex', to help her 'explain it the best way [she] can', the Woman uses the earth from the set as a prop, a visual aid, to map the skin laws she describes. Paired with light humour, this deepens the impact of her final movement, as she *'flays her arm through the remaining large pile and circle, destroying it'*. While the use of the prop is very concrete, the physical symbolism allows us to visualise something intricate, emotional and abstract. Another visual aid is the projection of the words in 'Wreck / con / silly / nation Poem'. While her lines convey the devastation of colonialism, the projections allow us to share her wordplay as she breaks down the word 'reconciliation' into words with very different connotations; by seeing this, we are forced to share the sadness the wordplay represents. Without the projection, the meaning of the scene would be lost. Visual projection is also used elsewhere in the play – sometimes in a relatively abstract form (such as the letters projected onto the Woman in 'Black Skin Girl') but often with a literal function, as with the family photographs. These images help to connect us with the Woman's family, recognising that they surround her emotionally and culturally just as the photographs surround her on the stage. In this way, multimodal elements emphasise important themes in the play – here, the vital role of family in identity and community.

Another way multimodal elements are used to amplify the themes and concerns of the play is by combining various forms of theatrical language; for example, in 'Sobbing', the pairing of sobbing (sound) with darkness (lighting) emphasises the scene's meaning. The darkness brings an increased vulnerability to the tears; together with the projection of the list of words, in this scene with no dialogue multimodal elements create a mood of sorrow and pain, which sets the tone for the rest of the play. Similarly, the scene 'Invasion Poem' invokes vulnerability in multiple ways. Firstly, the Woman uses poetry – which, as a mode, tends to be more figurative and subjective, thus exposing emotion that declarative language (such as in 'Mugshot') might resist. Secondly, the content of the poem is exceptionally raw, revealing deep pain through its metaphor. Thirdly, the Woman is still topless from the previous scene – a physical vulnerability that is arresting. Thus the multimodal forms of text in this scene combine to reiterate the idea of Indigenous peoples' vulnerability in the face of colonial invasion and contemporary conflict.

A secondary function of including rich multimodal content in the play is to create impactful contrast in scenes that do *not* have descriptive stage directions and multimedia components. Examples include 'Murri Gets a Dress', in which there are no sound effects, projections or props – this focuses attention directly on the Woman's daily experience. Similarly in 'Mugshot' the lack of any stagecraft directions startles us with the harshness of the events being described: this incident is concrete and does not need figurative interpretation. The lack of multimodal content at this point discourages audiences from making their own symbolic interpretations, instead forcing them to see the reality of the situation and confront such incidents.

Multimodal elements allow for themes and ideas to be emphasised without relying on the one-dimensional technique of simple verbal repetition. The inclusion of theatrical language such as stage directions, sound and projection not only situates *The 7 Stages of Grieving* within its multimodal genre, but facilitates a greater intellectual understanding of the play and a deeper emotional impact on the audience. Enoch and Mailman achieve this with a multimodal text that illustrates, supports and enhances the verbal elements of the play.

REFERENCES & READING

Text

Enoch, W & Mailman, D 2002, *The 7 Stages of Grieving*, 3rd edn, Playlab Press, Brisbane. First published 1996.

References

Bremer, R 2021, 'As *The 7 Stages of Grieving* is re-staged, Shari Sebbens and Elaine Crombie ask how much has changed in 26 years', *ABC News*, 5 June, https://www.abc.net.au/news/2021-06-05/the-7-stages-of-grieving-shari-sebbens-elaine-crombie/100178236

Casey, M & Craigie, C 2011, *A Brief History of Indigenous Australian Contemporary Theatre*, Australian Script Centre/AustralianPlays.org, Hobart, https://apt.org.au/assets/files/resource/doc/2012/06/BlakStage_Essay_ABriefHistory_DUPL_1.pdf

Dow, S 2021, '*The 7 Stages of Grieving* review – Elaine Crombie gives a singular performance in show that swings to outright activism', *The Guardian*, 26 May, https://www.theguardian.com/stage/2021/may/26/the-7-stages-of-grieving-review-elaine-crombie-gives-a-singular-performance-in-show-that-swings-to-outright-activism

Fanning, E 2019, 'One Plus One', *ABC News*, 24 January, https://www.abc.net.au/news/programs/one-plus-one/2019-01-24/one-plus-one:-wesley-enoch/10747450

Kübler-Ross, E 1969, *On Death and Dying*, Macmillan, New York.

Lucashenko, M 2015, '*The 7 Stages of Grieving*', Reading Australia, Copyright Agency, https://readingaustralia.com.au/essays/the-7-stages-of-grieving/

Pryor, S 2021, 'The latest version of Deborah Mailman's play *The 7 Stages of Grieving* end with a new message of hope', *The Canberra Times*, 24 June, https://www.canberratimes.com.au/story/7310730/messages-of-hope-amid-the-grief/

Zhou, D 2021, 'Review of *The 7 Stages of Grieving*', *Time Out*, 27 May, https://www.timeout.com/sydney/theatre/the-7-stages-of-grieving-1